AGGLOMERATIVE SUBCENTERS
IN
MONOCENTRIC
CITIES

by

JOHN F. SASE, Ph.D.

AGGLOMERATIVE SUBCENTERS IN MONOCENTRIC CITIES

THE DEVELOPMENT OF AGGLOMERATIVE SUBCENTERS
IN RADIAL MONOCENTRIC CITIES

By
John F. Sase, Ph.D.

Senior Editor: Gerard J. Senick

ISBN-13: 978-1491061169

ISBN-10: 1491061162

Address inquiries to
drjohn@saseassociates.com
SASE Associates, LLC

TABLE OF CONTENTS

For Julie

whose patience, encouragement, and support

helped see this to completion

Special thanks, for guidance, to

Allen C. Goodman
Ralph M. Braid
Robert W. Wasmer
Robert Sinclair
Edwin S. Mills
John F. Kain
&
others who have peered
through the same oculus

LIST OF TABLES

LIST OF FIGURES

PREFACE

This volume explores the development of the monocentric urban model. Throughout the following chapters, the history of the concept, the development of the general model, and the creation of a specific model, which includes subcenters, are considered. Next, the specific model is tested against business-census data for ten radial monocentric cities in the United States. Results and implications are reported. Finally, a survey of research that grew out of the initial research and that has extended from the date of the initial project through the present time is presented. Chapters 1 through 5 contain the development of the spine of the research. Chapter 6 contains a brief of major research elements built upon the spine.

CHAPTER I

I. INTRODUCTION

There has been an increase in agglomerative subcentering over the past four decades in many large metropolitan areas. What present society describes as urban sprawl or suburban flight may simply be a natural process of urban-regional development, consistent with monocentric urban thought and development extending backwards in time for more than two millennia. By objective, the theoretical work of this book emulates major monocentric models developed over the past three millennia to develop an extended mathematical model with agglomerative subcenters. Next, the empirical work tests this extended model against observations of Major Retail Centers (MRCs) for radially monocentric SMSAs. Through a two-step econometric technique which includes a model-specification error test, the results ascertain the existence and locations of peak subcenter activity at an average of approximately half the distance from the Central Business District to the furthest MRC. This position concurs with Plato's ideal model of Magnesia and other works of the past three millennia.

Fundamentally, the inspiration and intuition for this book comes from a lifetime of oral and written cultural tradition. Building upon this tradition, this work uses the historical chronicles and analyses found in Chapter 2 to develop the theoretical model in Chapter 3. In retrospect, the empirical Results, in Chapter 4, support the theory of peak subcenter activity developed in Chapter 3.

II. THE HISTORICAL WORK

The literature which forms the background for this book can be divided into three major areas: historical origin, theoretical development, and empirical testing. Chapter 2 traces the historical origins of the monocentric urban models which justify the development of agglomerative employment subcenters. The history asserts that monocentric urban-regional models may have roots that are more ancient than previously reported. Though Samuelson [89] and others trace the monocentric model back to *The Isolated State* of Von Thünen [97, 98, 99], evidence of monocentric urban models and monocentric sites exists which dates from before the time of Plato. This chapter traces the monocentric urban concept in western thought and by so doing provides material with which to extend the Standard Urban Model. In addition, this chapter also uncovers ancient variations to the concentric-ring model including radial pathways and employment subcenters.

The literature on the historical origins in Chapter 2 comes from inter-disciplinary sources. It lends support to an extensive tradition of monocentric urban thought. More specifically, this literature extends backwards in time by more than two millennia. It lends historical support to the theory of agglomerative subcenters used in the present theoretical model and empirical testing. The literature employed to develop the primitive origins of monocentric cities primarily comes from the fields of anthropology, archaeology, and philosophy. The treatment of Middle Eastern roots draws in works from the fields of religious and cultural studies. The section on the culmination of monocentric urban thought in ancient Greece includes the writings of Plato and commentaries on Plato by modern writers. The literature relevant to thought during the early Christian era includes scriptural sources, early religious writings and modern commentaries on these writings. The modern development of the model includes earlier models found in the utopian literature of the age of enlightenment and later models which stem from the utopian tradition, enveloping modern economic thought. Current models, following the earlier tradition, are described in the standard present day economic literature which form the basis for the extended model developed in the theory chapter.

The purpose of the historical research is to chronicle the evolution of monocentric thought and provide material with which to generate an extended standard urban model in Chapter 3. In response to the development of major urban subcenters in recent decades, the need exists for revised models, consistent with the existent standard model, that sufficiently address recent urban growth issues.

The general evolution of monocentric thought uncovers a number of ancient variations. A number of ancient variations are useful in developing revised models. A few of these variations are used to develop the revised model in Chapter 3.

III. THE THEORETICAL WORK

Three areas of monocentric literature lend themselves to the development of the theoretical model in Chapter 3. These areas include monocentric models in general, urban employment subcenters, and agglomeration economies as applicable to subcenters. In respect to monocentric models in general, ancient works including those of Plato, John of Patmos, and St. Augustine, medieval works including those of St. Thomas More and Campanella, and the modern works of Von Thünen [97, 98, 99], Howard [41], Park and Burgess [75], Lösch [50, 51, 52], Alonso [2, 3, 4], and Mills [64, 65, 66, 67, 68] provide the basis for the development of the extended model. The works of McDonald and Bowman [62] and others further support the use of the negative-exponential function and similar measures for determining urban gradients.

Moses and Williamson [72], White [102], Tauchen and Witte [93], MaCauley [54], and Yinger [104] directly address the issue of suburbanization of employment, business subcentering, and agglomeration economies. Moses and Williamson more specifically address the issue of subcentering in respect to the minimization of transportation costs. White presents evidence for the existence of employment subcenters. Tauchen and Witte discuss the issue agglomeration economies in application to business centers. MaCauley updates the work of Mills specifically including suburbanization of retailing relevant to this work. Yinger carries his analysis of business centers to three-dimensional space including the use of the double integral function (which is similarly used in the current model developed in Chapter 3).

Chapter 3 develops an urban model with an employment center and subcenters resulting from bidding among competing users and from agglomeration economies. Generally, urban models consider rent only with respect the radial dimension. However in this model, competitive bidding between business and residences for urban land leads to an analysis of rent with respect to both the radial and lateral dimensions in a monocentric city expressed in a polar coordinate space. This city emulates Plato's allegorical city of Magnesia and other ideal urban models reviewed in Chapter 2. The city has a small number of equidistant radial highways extending from the Central Business District (CBD). A large but finite number of streets laterally cross the highways. Commuters and transporters choose the radial highway that minimizes travel costs to off-highway locations. As a result, they generally limit travel to one of the uniform radial segments. Therefore, the process of subcentering can be analyzed and generalized from one radial segment.

The first part of the chapter develops a simple model of land allocation through competitive bidding. Bidding, among land users, results in a business area concentrated around the CBD, tapering outward along the radial highway. The analysis d from the standard urban model with the introduction of compound lateral bid-rent functions for both business and residential users. The combination of a negatively-sloped normal business bid-rent function and a very steep negatively-sloped premium-bid function for highway frontage produces a negatively sloped upper-envelope lateral bid-rent curve. However, subtracting a negative-exponential disamenity residential bid-rent function from a normal negative-exponential function produces a lateral residential bid-rent curve. This curve, which initially has a positive slope, reaches a maximum a short distance from the highway and then becomes negatively sloped thereafter. This results in land apportionment to the dominant bidder at each point location. Bidding apportions all land near the CBD to business. However, increasing percentages of land go to residential users at further distances from the CBD. This bidding apportionment produces a business center that tapers out along the radial highway.

The second part of the chapter develops a subcenter case of land allocation through competitive bidding. The bid-rent profile changes through the introduction of an avoidance-rent phase to the radial dimension of the residential bid-rent surface. The avoidance-rent segment has a positive slope at intermediate distances. As a result, change in competitive bidding reallocates land. This reallocation produces a business subcenter close to the urban limit.

The final part of the chapter analyzes the effect of agglomeration economies on subcenter development. Assuming a minimum critical size (Richardson, [86]) for the subcenter, an adaptation of the Weber [100] agglomeration model introduces the process of agglomeration economies to subcenter development. With this introduction, an increase of subcenter area and a local maximum on the business bid-rent surface occurs at the center of agglomeration. These occurrences remain consistent with the findings of White [102] and Yinger [104].

IV. THE EMPIRICAL WORK

The literature concerned with the empirical testing of the monocentric model with agglomerative subcenters fall into two general areas. The first includes generally available econometric techniques. The second contains econometric techniques specific to this genre of urban economic analysis. Fundamentally, the econometric analysis uses a classical regression model of the log-linear form of a negative-exponential function with linear restrictions. The use of the employment density function has been drawn from the work of McDonald and Bowman [62] who test four proxy density measurements and provides support and justification for the use of employment density as a suitable measure for identifying subcenters. More directly, this work follows the work of Dubin and Sung [19] which uses a spline function to address the spatial variation in the price of housing, and the work of Goodman and Dubin [34] and Goodman and Dubin [35] in the general testing and similar application of the Davidson and MacKinnon [18] model-specification error test (J-test).

Given data for ten SMSAs, a comparative t-test, and a Davidson-MacKinnon J-test are used to ascertain the existence and location of peak retail subcenter activity. This study executes these tests alternately for employment density and gross sales density. It follows from the model and hypothesis developed in sections II and III of Chapter 4, that one peak of subcenter activity should occur at distance μ^{**} miles from the Central Business District (CBD). Furthermore, peak subcenter activity should occur at a short lateral distance ρ^{**} miles from a radial highway. Therefore in both the employment and gross sales density functions, evidence of radial and lateral locations of peak subcenter activity should appear as local radial and lateral maxima.

The average distances of the employment and sales peaks occur midway between the CBD and the furthest MRC. Results for employment density indicate that peak activity occurs at an average of .51 of that radial distance. At this peak, average estimated density is 1.7 times the average employment density at the CBD. Furthermore, results for the sales density studies have indicated that peak activity occurs at an average of .52 of the radial distance. However, at the sales peak, average estimated density is 3.4 times the average sales density at the CBD.

CHAPTER 2

I. INTRODUCTION

Monocentric urban-regional models may have roots more ancient than previously reported. Samuelson [89] and others trace the monocentric model back to *The Isolated State* of Von Thünen [97, 98, 99]. However, evidence exists which dates monocentric urban models and monocentric urban sites from primitive times. Later, ancient monocentric urban thought reached an apex in Greece. Plato developed a set of monocentric urban allegories based on a mathematical tradition which may date back to the Sumero-Babylonian period. This Platonic tradition and a number of other prominent ancient traditions survived throughout the Middle-Ages and appear to have influenced a line of monocentric urban thought which began during the Renaissance and continues to this day.

This chapter has a two-fold purpose. First, the chronicling of the evolution of the monocentric urban concept in Western thought and practice offers to the field of economics a deeper historical foundation supporting the relevance of monocentric models. Next, the research provides substantiated material with which to extend the Standard Urban Model. Consistent with the existent model, the need exists for revised models that sufficiently address recent urban growth issues such as the development of major urban manufacturing, service, and retail subcenters in recent decades that often overshadow older central business districts.

In tracing the evolution of monocentric urban-regional thought from ancient times to the present, this chapter also uncovers a number of ancient variations of the monocentric model which may prove useful for model revision.

The monocentric model stands as one of many urban models. Lynch [53] presents the range of general urban models including the star (monocentric radial), the linear city, and the rectangular city. Lynch implies that a sole universal urban model does not exist because cities develop in a number of distinctly different ways. However, the monocentric model does form the basis of the Standard Urban Model as developed by Lösch, Mills, and others.

As stated, the field usually traces modern monocentric urban-regional models back to *The Isolated State* of Von Thünen. In this tradition, monocentric models (also known as modern concentric-zone urban land use models) are generally described as a central urban area surrounded by a number of employment and residential rings. However, evidence exists of much earlier locational models that bear striking similarities to contemporary models. These ancient monocentric models often include features such as radial pathways and employment subcenters--a feature not always found in modern models. Indeed, these earlier models predate the work of Von Thünen by more than two millennia. Therefore, antiquarian sources for this meta-history of the monocentric urban model draw from a range of sources, including the fields of anthropology, archeology, history, philosophy, and religious studies.

II. PRIMITIVE ROOTS OF MONOCENTRIC THOUGHT

Though the ancient monocentric models reached a culmination in development and a refinement in technique during the Greek classical age, the legacy of these ancient models can be traced to the era of pre-history. The mathematical tools available to the ancient Greeks form the foundation for the formulation of modern models. Plato and other ancients appear to have derived monocentric spatial models from the ever-growing reservoir of mathematics, symbols, myths, and elementary ideas. Not only do the ancient and modern models appear to have an elementary numerical foundation in the development of their stories, but they also employ the circle, triangle, and cone (vortex) as a basis for allegory. In this use, these mathematical concepts appear to have roots in ancient mythology. Joseph Campbell [13] indicates that there is every reason to believe that this ancient mythology (into which, at some unknown date, accurate numerical insight was introduced) dates to the Sumero-Babylonian period, or possibly earlier.

Eliade [20] offers to urban studies an underlying raison d'etre for the existence of monocentric cities. He accomplishes this by presenting many examples from both primitive and traditional societies.

Eliade states that because traditional cultures believe that human beings need holy sites to form the center of a settlement, the principal cosmological image across cultures has been a cosmic pillar supporting heaven. It is from this pillar that a sequence of conceptions and images emerges that forms a system of the world. A sacred place breaks the homogeneity of space. This break constitutes an axis around which our world is located. From this point, Eliade surmises that this axis forms the center of the world. He further states that this center is often represented by a real or mythical mountain. Analogous to these mountains, holy sites such as mounds, temples and churches are believed to be situated at the center of the world.

According to Eliade, traditional societies characteristically reflect this macrocosm in the microcosm as they reiterate this image of the world on increasingly smaller scales through a multiplicity of centers. The cosmogony of traditional cultures forms the paradigmatic model for their every construction. By this principle, the settling of a territory is equivalent to the founding of a world.

Buildings also have roots in the transcendent. On the most microcosmic level, Eliade states that cosmic symbolism appears in the structure of housing. The tent or house constitutes an image of the world. This follows from the primitive belief that traditional cultures conceive of the sky as a vast tent supported by a central pillar of the world. Not only can one consider a modern city as a microcosm of the world, but three-dimensional renderings of the modern model actually resemble such a tent (Lösch, [51]).

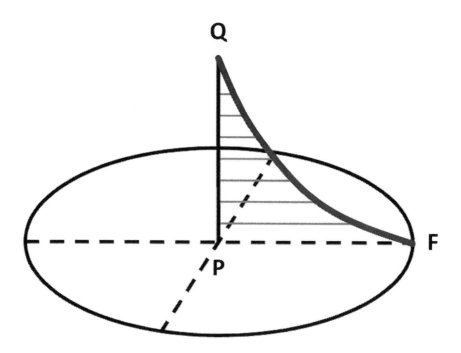

Fig. 1a. Lösch, Fig. 21

Therefore, Eliade concludes that traditional societies derive symbols and rituals having to do with temples, cities, and houses from the primary experience of sacred space. This theme, which has endured throughout history and across cultures, forms the common thread running throughout the early evolution of the monocentric urban model.

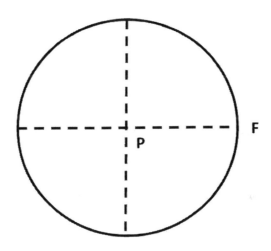

Fig. 1b. Lösch, Fig. 21, Top View

III. MONOCENTRICITY IN HISTORY

A. MONOCENTRIC CULMINATION IN GREEK THOUGHT

It seems that earlier Greek monocentric cosmologies such as those of Anaximander and Parmenides inspired Plato's monocentric urban models. Furley [29, 30] presents the Greek cosmologies of Anaximander and Parmenides that provide the models for understanding the social and economic relations of ancient Greek culture. However, Plato applies these models in conjunction with the mathematics communicated by Pythagoras to create his mathematical allegories of the perfect city-state.[1]

Plato's models are, essentially, mathematical allegories. Brumbaugh [10] states that much of the work which the early Greek philosophers and scientists thought of as mathematics is not "mathematics" in its twentieth-century form at all. However, their fundamental concepts of algebra, proportions, and geometry form the basis of contemporary mathematics.[2] The ratio theories of Plato's Academy translate into modern exponential functions and often represent special cases of general formulae (Fowler

---

[1] It appears that Pythagoras introduced the analytical tools used by Plato to ancient Greece. The germane aspects of his teachings can be traced back to the Sumero-Babylonian age of the previous millenium (Neugebauer [74].)

[2] In this century, efforts have been made to search for common-sense implications in Plato's mathematical allegories. The work of various leading Platonists, including Adam [1], Taylor [94], and Cornford [14,15], led Brumbaugh [10,11] to advance the theory that the "mathematical" passages in Plato's work, which scholars had considered nonsense or riddles in earlier centuries, actually describe diagrams designed by the philosopher, intended to accompany and clarify his text.

[24]). This body of ancient mathematics suffices for the construction of Plato's allegorical city-states.

Plato constructs four allegorical city-states: ancient Athens, an ideal one; modern Athens (Calliopolis), also ideal but inhabited by only an essential population; Atlantis, a luxurious one of destructive excesses; and Magnesia, the practicable city-state.

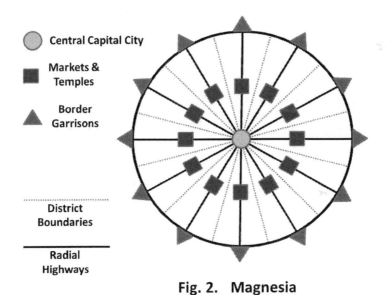

Fig. 2. Magnesia

McClain [58] states that Plato constructs his allegorical city-states from abstract material developed in earlier mathematical allegories. The Myth of Er contains Plato's cosmological model embodied in the Spindle of Necessity. The allegory of the Spindle expounds on mathematical concepts, essential for understanding Plato's four city-state models found in later writings. In the *Republic* [79], Plato describes the Spindle of Necessity as having a center column which appears as a straight shaft of light that stretches from above throughout heaven and earth. The Spindle of Necessity represents the dynamics of the universe. Furthermore, he describes a set of eight bowl-shaped whorls (convex hulls). These whorls spin about the vertical shaft of light that extends infinitely upward and downward through the bottom center of all the bowls. The mathematical allegory of the Spindle of Necessity resembles the cosmological image which Eliade [20] associates with the village construction rituals of primitive and traditional societies.

The Spindle of Necessity embodies a curvilinear mathematical function, fundamental to city-state allegories of Plato, which approximates the negative-exponential function used by Mills and other modern-age model builders. The bridge between the Spindle and the negative exponential functions is the diatonic musical scale such that musical pitches, expressed as cycles per second, graph as a convex curvilinear function. McClain [59] details the correlations between the musical scale and the nested whorls in the Spindle of Necessity in respect to the shape of the whorls, the width of the rims, the patterns of the colors, the speeds, and other relevant aspects. This body of harmonic mathematics forms the essential tools which Plato uses to construct his allegories.

The concept of monocentricity is germane to Plato's urban allegories. He establishes this concept in other allegories through the ideas of circularity and axis. Plato reveals that the circle constitutes his own primary image (*Timaeus* [81]). From this, it follows that his cities are circular.

In the *Republic*, Plato [78] begins his development of an ideal model state with a one-dimensional line which evolves into a two-dimensional circle. James Adam [1] interpreted these passages as the state growing like a circle drawn with a compass. As a result, the state as a circle forms the fundamental ground plan for all of Plato's city-state models. As a circle drawn with a compass, pivoting at the center, all these models are monocentric.

In effect, Plato creates four variations of a monocentric city-state. Each has a seat of power at its center: Both ancient and new Athens has a temple of Zeus; Atlantis has the palace of Poseidon; and Magnesia has its capital city, the seat of its government.

Throughout ancient times, land transportation remained essentially limited to foot and horse travel. As a result of transportation modes that are expensive in physical and time costs, the preference for residence and occupation tended to be close to the city center. Due to these high physical and time costs, employment and housing sectors tended to be integrated in the sense that citizens lived where they worked.[3]

Plato describes how the social hierarchy of the city-states imply declining wage and rent gradients. He offers an example in the allegory of Athens.

---

[3] Moses and Williamson [72], in their study of the transition from the horse-and-wagon age to the motor-truck age, present the thesis that the cost of moving goods was high relative to the cost of moving people within cities in the nineteenth century. Even if this same cost relationship held during the time of Plato, the output per acre of the trade good compared to the output per acre of housing production would have been much lower in pre-industrial times such that

$$(t_1 - t_2)/t_2 < a_2/a_1$$

would hold. This inequality condition for integration of work and residence locations (where t_1 represents cost per unit per mile of moving goods, t_2 represents cost per mile of moving a worker, a_1 represents output per acre of the trade good, and a_2 represents output per acre of housing production) implies that integration is more efficient than segregation if it cheaper to move goods than people or if product per acre of housing production is sufficiently greater than output per acre of the trade good (Mills [67]).

"...Hephaestos and Athene (the children of Zeus),...produced a native race of good men and gave them suitable political arrangements....on (the) immediate slopes (of Athens) lived the craftsmen and the agricultural workers who worked in the neighbourhood. Higher up the military class lived by itself round the temple of Athena and Hephaestos [80]."

In Athens, Plato has set his society in three class levels. The wealthy ruling class sits figuratively and literally at the top center. Halfway down the mountain, the military holds a mid-ring position. At the base, the agricultural and industrial classes form the outermost circle.[4] This segment of the allegory precurses contemporary studies which have examined the degree of suburbanization of various employment sectors (Mills, [66], MaCauley, [54]).

The physical gradient of socio-economic classes appears typical of urban societies until recent times. Well water tends to have greater contamination in low-lying areas. As a result, the upper-class has almost always built its housing on high ground (Mills and Hamilton, [69]). It is only with improved pure water supply and sewage disposal technologies of the past century that enormous health problems, resulting from increased density of

---

[4] Plato [80,82] describes Atlantis and Magnesia as being close to level in appearance. However, the social structures are similar to those of the two Athens, implying similar wage, and rent gradients.

population in cities, have been solved (Glaab and Brown, [31]). Thus, partially due to improved public health, higher income groups have changed their location preferences.

Land use in the four city-states takes two different forms. Athens, divided into two semi-circles, is a mountain split into residential and occupational faces. By contrast, Plato describes Atlantis as six concentric rings of alternating water and land which surround the central island [80].

Magnesia brings together both elements. The practicable state consists of two concentric rings around the central city (fig. 2). Plato divides the surrounding agricultural land into twelve quasi-equal radial segments by six diagonals [82].

In his allegory of Magnesia, Plato [82] constructs a practicable city-state. Brumbaugh [11] writes that Plato locates the central city in the most efficient way, in respect to its territory, for purposes of administration, defense, and trade. This radial plan proves the most efficient for long-haul transportation from the perimeter of Magnesia to the capital city. The central city in this plan is a center of symmetry.

Plato states that the legislator must first locate the city as precisely as possible in the center of the country. In terms of public choice, citizens will remain economically indifferent as to location around the circular state. Secondly, the legislator must divide the circular country into twelve sections. This symmetry provides for public choice equilibrium among all sections.[5] Plato continues to describe the physical layout of Magnesia which Brumbaugh [11] presents in his Map of Magnesia. Extending radially from the central-capital city, the seat of government services, twelve highways run to the boundary. This boundary, protected by border garrisons, may emerge as a secondary employment subcenter. As with military bases throughout history, businesses providing goods and services of many kinds would experience agglomeration economies by locating near the garrisons.

However, the primary employment subcenters exist further inland. McClain [57] describes Magnesia as a double ring. Halfway along the radial roads, at the bound of the inner ring, exist twelve temple/market areas. These temple/market areas have emerged as employment subcenters in the land of Magnesia. In modern times, the market areas take the form of retail centers.

---

[5] Actual cities, such as Detroit, London, Moscow, and Paris have developed economically in radial segments (Sinclair [91] and Hall [38]).

The modern expression of the ancient Greek form appears as the small town in the midst of an agricultural region. In these towns, society divides the function of the temple between the church and district school. The market may simply appear as a general store, a livery or gas station, and perhaps a tavern, movie house, or bowling alley. This subcenter may provide virtually all of the non-agricultural private sector employment in the region.

In analyzing the models presented above, it seems that the allegorical city-states of Plato provide the most sophisticated and detailed models of ancient thought. Though Plato did not have the power of modern mathematics at his disposal, he did provide us with thorough verbal descriptions of various human relationships in an ideal society. Using the system of harmonic mathematics known to many ancient intellects, Plato also produced a series of monocentric urban models having both implied and physical gradients. These models embodied standard features such as division by concentric rings, division by diagonals, and agglomerative subcenters. Division by multiple concentric rings appears in numerous models from the earliest to the most modern including those of Von Thünen [97,98], and Mills [65]. Agglomerative subcenters appear recently in the work of White [102].[6] Division of space into numerous radial segments (primarily six and twelve) appears in numerous models before and after Plato. However, there has been less use of this modeling technique in recent centuries.

C. EARLY CHRISTIAN ERA
THROUGH THE RENAISSANCE.

Through the allegorical city-states of Plato exemplify the most thoroughly developed of those represented in ancient thought, they are by no means unique. The cosmogony and inherent mathematical system from which Plato drew appear to have been understood throughout the ancient world. The last major expression in terms of an ideal urban model appeared at the time of transition from the Greco-Roman to Magian period in the work of John of Patmos. Even during the Middle Ages when ancient Greek thought fell into obscurity, the ideal monocentric city described by John of Patmos continued to influence Western thought.

In his *Apocalypse,* John of Patmos presents the evolution of an ideal city. He describes the center with a majestic figure on a

---

[6] Richardson [86] surveys the literature of agglomeration economies.

throne, and the center surrounded by a court [42, 43]. This description implies a centralized government service sector.

Around this throne is gathered a population of twenty-four elders. John [44] next describes an extended population of thousands surrounding the twenty-four. He then partitions this multitude into twelve segments and divides the whole population into two classes [45]. The first class of two-thirds of the whole is to be saved, while the second class of one-third is to be destroyed [46].

The image of the heavenly city, from the Greek and Christian golden age, may have survived the medieval world for political rather than aesthetic reasons. Following the capture of Rome in 410 A.D. by the Goths, a fear existed within the Christian Church that the citizens of Rome would blame the Church for the collapse of the empire resulting in a return by the Roman people to the old religions and to martial and heroic values. In response, the Church distinguished The City of Man from the City of God, thereby separating church from state, and giving each separate but related spheres of operation (Augustine [5]). As a result, the simpler monocentric model of John of Patmos (also believed by many to be one of the twelve Apostles of Christ) survived in art and literature as the principal expression of the ideal city until the late Middle-Ages. This ideal city of John of Patmos most closely resembles the structure of Plato's land of Magnesia.

D. THE MODERN AGE

During the Dark Ages, which followed the fall of the Roman empire, much ancient knowledge becomes lost or submerged in Western culture. Toward the end of the Middle-Ages, Thomas Aquinas and other scholars re-introduce Plato's ideas into mainstream Western thought, events which led to the rebirth of monocentric urban thought during the Renaissance.

New developments in the monocentric urban model come during the first phase of the Renaissance with Thomas More's writing of *Utopia*. More creates a utopia that is not a paradise myth, but rather a vehicle for comments on his own society. More uses his model in a way similar to modern economic models.

In *Utopia*, More [70, 71] creates a circular island with a central island separated from an outer ring by a circular river. From a mountain, adjacent to the bay at one side of the island, the river runs around the inner island and empties into the bay, thereby separating the island into two rings. More locates the principal city at the center of the island and seven smaller settlements around the outer ring.

Generally, More contributes to the development of the monocentric model in the Platonic tradition by re-introducing to Western thought the use of an allegorical land to build an extensive analysis of social mechanism. Specifically, Thomas More offers a number of social plans with economic ramifications. Within the territory of any city, he allows a completely mobile labor force to journey to any location, practice their trade, and be accepted by others of the same trade. More provides this mobile labor force with free use of an oxen drawn wagon driven by a public slave. During his journey the laborer carries nothing with him for he feels at home everywhere. This transportation system reduces the private physical costs to zero and ensures that no external costs arise due to lack of familiar neighborhood amenities.

Between the time of More and Von Thünen, a number of ideal-city models appear including those of Campanella [12] and Ledoux [49] (who selects a real plan site). Most of these early models concern themselves with elements of public sector economics and the government service sector which would regulate all private sector activity.

In the tradition of Plato and his successors, Von Thünen [97, 98] develops a model with a central town surrounded by six concentric agricultural rings and like Ledoux, Von Thünen selects a real plan site (though his site is the bleak terrain of northern Germany). However, using land rent, wage, and profit theories developed by Adam Smith and other earlier classical economists, Von Thünen addresses the economic aspects of the monocentric state in more precise language than had earlier monocentrists (Von Thünen [99]).

Similar to Plato's Athens and Magnesia, Von Thünen imagines his state as having only one very large town at the center of a fertile plain. No rivers or canals exist. The cultivatable plain is of homogenous fertility. Surrounding this circular state lays an uncultivated wilderness which isolates the state. Mines near the town supply raw material for the manufacturers who all locate in town. Von Thünen devotes the surrounding plain to agriculture.

Von Thünen describes this agrarian area as six differentiated concentric rings (fig. 3). From the innermost outward, he describes their uses for free cash cropping, forestry, a crop rotation system, a second form of crop rotation that is less intensive than the previous ring, a three fallow system, and the grazing of animals. Rent decreases from the center outward, as does population density.

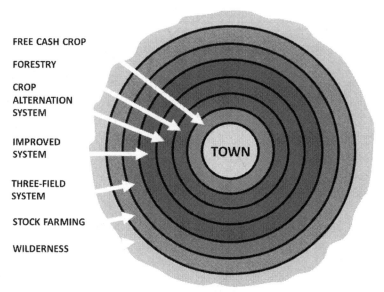

FREE CASH CROP

FORESTRY

CROP ALTERNATION SYSTEM

IMPROVED SYSTEM

THREE-FIELD SYSTEM

STOCK FARMING

WILDERNESS

TOWN

Fig. 3. The Isolated State

Similar economic situations exist for both Plato and Von Thünen. Their world functions by foot and horse-drawn transportation. Von Thünen concerns himself not with the economics of intra-urban manufacturing transportation, but rather agricultural transportation, which has the more significant effect upon land rents in a world of concentrated urban areas.

Later in the century, following in the path of Robert Owen, Henry George, and Edward Bellamy, Ebenezer Howard [41] creates a utopian garden city (*Garden Cities of Tomorrow*) (fig. 4). To the development of the monocentric model, he contributes explicit delineations of acreage and population which provide a model for the study of population and employment densities in both a central city and in smaller subcenters as a model for urban growth. In a manner reminiscent of Plato's Magnesia, he sets forth a plan for a central city that has grown to the dimensions of 12,000 acres and a population of 58,000 which connects by a radial system of canals to six sub-cities, each with an area of 9,000 acres and a population of 32,000. A canal encircles the central city. Howard divides the remainder of the territory into two concentric rings by another circular canal which connects the six sub-cities to one another as seen in his "No. 7: Group of Slumless Smokeless Cities." The central city has the denser population of 3,072 residents per square mile compared to 2,240 persons per square mile in each of the six sub-cities.

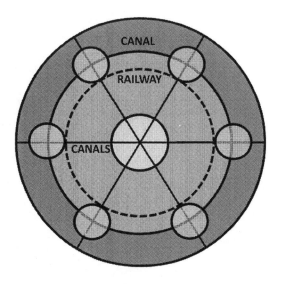

Fig. 4.   Garden City No. 7

Of the four modern models discussed thus far, three address the transportation problem of cross-hauling. Thomas More employs a circular river as a means of minimizing cross-haul transportation costs subject to the condition of serving all outlying regions equally.   Howard offers the most thorough solution to the problem by using both land and water transportation. With a circular inter-municipal canal between the six sub-cities and a circular inter-municipal railway closer to the central city, Howard solves this constrained minimization problem using the two lowest weight-cost-per-mile transportation modes known in his time.

Park and Burgess [75] set the stage for the development of current monocentric urban models. They develop a monocentric growth model for any city. At the center they locate the Central Business District (the loop). Surrounding the CBD exists a zone in transition. Park and Burgess describe the inner portion of this ring as a factory zone. Third exists the zone of workingmen's homes. The distinction between the second and third rings implies a segregation of employment locations from residences in a way that precurses Mills [65]. This appears as the modern foundation of an alternative non-agglomerative subcenter model.

The work of Lösch [50] forms another intermediary step between the models of Von Thünen and Mills. In his Economics of Location, Lösch develops a system based on Von Thünen's theory and refers to him in discussing the advantages of belts of locations producing identical goods. In figures 20-21 of his book, Lösch presents a visual model of a monocentric market with a declining (mill) price gradient (fig. 5). He defines the featureless plain by a pair of axis. The price of grain declines from Q to P as the market expands radially from the origin to point F at the perimeter. This model, having its graph in the form of a nomadic tent in Eliade's description of a traditional society in section II of this chapter, provides another foundation for the model of Mills.

In his discussion of the system of networks, Lösch [52] describes a theoretical pattern of an economic landscape with and without nets in his figures 28 and 29. Here he describes a monocentric model with a central city surrounded by two metropolitan rings containing 102 sub-cities distributed among twelve radial segments. Again, this modern model resembles the Magnesia of Plato and other ancient ones.

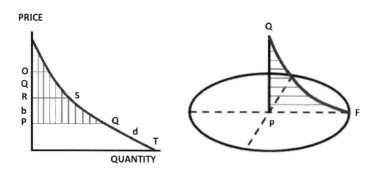

Fig. 5.   Lösch, Fig. 20 and 21

Alonso [2, 3, 4] forms a bridge between Lösch and Mills by developing a rigorous mathematical approach to locational equilibrium. His mathematical solutions for individual equilibrium, equilibrium of the firm, and a simultaneous equations solution for individual and market equilibrium appear particularly interesting.

Mills [68] constructs a circular model of urban structure with a predetermined center, ϕ available radians, and $2\pi - \phi$ unavailable radians (which may be a swamp or harbor). He describes both the central business district and residential area as being semicir-cular--a concept especially applicable to Chicago and Detroit and other monocentric cities. In addition, he also employs the curvilinear negative-exponential function as a predictor of rental, wage, and profit gradients.

If one introduces subcenters, says Mills [66], there will exist some completely segregated central city employment and some employment partly integrated with residential activity. White [102] and McDonald [60] extend this feature of the Mills model in their analysis of urban subcenters (fig. 6). The importance of subcenters has been noted in the earlier modern work of Howard as well as Plato's Magnesia. Similar to Plato's Magnesia and Howard's Garden Cities, Dubin and Sung [19], Yinger [104] and others use radial pie-shaped segments to address the issue of suburbanization.

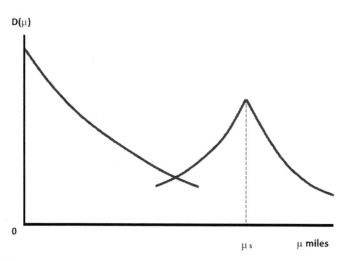

Fig. 6. Urban Subcenter

Essentially, the model of Mills updates the locational work of Lösch and Alonso. For this reason, his model of employment and population location within a monocentric city serves as the springboard for specific application model developed in chapter 3. This new variation incorporates a variety of concepts found in the many ideal models and numerous real monocentric cities discussed here.

IV. CONCLUSION

Throughout the ages, monocentric urban models have provided civilizations with useful tools for self-analysis and have provided the foundation for developing new models in succeeding ages. Though these models have changed from age to age, certain themes, such as radiating roads and concentric urban rings, have continued to reappear throughout the evolution of the models. The analyses contained within vary from the prose of Plato, More, and Von Thünen to the mathematics of Lösch, Alonso, and Mills. However, they all provide material for the development of the model in Chapter 3.

In conclusion, a new stage in the evolution of the monocentric model appears. This present research suggests a revised standard model having three principal features: a circular plain with a centralized primary business district, a radial partitioning of land, and a surrounding ring with agglomerative subcenters located at nodal points along this ring. The following chapter develops a revised urban model based on these principal features.

CHAPTER 3

I. INTRODUCTION

This chapter creates an urban model of employment centers and subcenters resulting from bidding among competing users, and from agglomeration economies. Generally, urban models consider rent only with respect to one physical dimension. However in this model, competitive bidding between business and residences for urban land leads to an analysis of rent with respect to two physical dimensions in a monocentric city expressed in a polar coordinate space. This city emulates Plato's allegorical city of Magnesia and other ideal urban models developed in Chapter 2. The city has a small number of equidistant radial highways extending from the Central Business District (CBD). A large but finite number of streets laterally cross the highways. Commuters and transporters choose the radial highway that minimizes travel costs to off-highway locations. As a result, they generally limit travel to one of the uniform radial segments. Therefore, the process of subcentering can be analyzed and generalized from one radial segment.

The first part of the chapter develops a simple model of land allocation through competitive bidding. Initially, bidding among users results in a business area concentrated around the CBD, tapering outward along the radial highway. The analysis departs from the standard urban model with the introduction of compound lateral bid-rent functions for both business and residential users. The combination of a negatively-sloped normal business bid-rent function and a very steep negatively-sloped premium-bid function for highway frontage produces a negatively sloped upper-envelope lateral bid-rent curve.

However, subtracting a negative-exponential disamenity residential bid-rent function from a normal negative-exponential function produces a lateral residential bid-rent curve. This curve, which initially has a positive slope, reaches a maximum at a short distance from the highway, and then becomes negatively sloped thereafter. This results in land apportionment to the dominant bidder at each point location. Bidding apportions all land near the CBD to business. However, increasing percentages of land go to residential users at further distances from the CBD. This bidding apportionment produces a business center that tapers out along the radial highway.

The second part of the chapter develops a subcenter case of land allocation through competitive bidding. The bid-rent profile changes through the introduction of an avoidance-rent phase to the radial dimension of the residential bid-rent surface. The avoidance-rent segment has a positive slope at intermediate distances. As a result, change in competitive bidding leads to a reallocation of land. This reallocation produces a business subcenter close to the urban limit.

The final part of the chapter analyzes the effect of agglomeration economies on subcenter development. Assuming a minimum critical size (Richardson [86]) for the subcenter, an adaptation of the Weber [100] agglomeration model introduces the process of agglomeration economies to subcenter development. With this introduction, an increase of subcenter area and a local maximum on the business bid-rent surface occurs at the center of agglomeration. These results remain consistent with the findings of White [102] and Yinger [104].

II. BIDDING BETWEEN BUSINESS
AND RESIDENTIAL USERS

The first part of the chapter develops a simple model of land allocation through competitive bidding. Initially, bidding among users results in a business area concentrated around the CBD, tapering outward along the radial highway.

Competitive bidding occurs between business and residential users for locations within the urban limit such that a radial distance of μ miles is less than the distance of the urban limit μ *bar*. Earlier research indicates a steeper bid-rent gradient for business sectors than for the residential sector (Mills [65]). As a result, business outbids residential users for locations close to the CBD.

Yinger contends that an urban model containing a finite number of radial highways more closely resembles reality than do models with an infinite number of highways. In accord with Yinger, this model contains a finite number of radial highways.

In the simple case that follows, negative-exponential functions approximate both the business and residential bid-rents. However, though a simple negative-exponential expresses the lateral dimension of the business function, a compound function resulting from the difference between two simple negative-exponential functions expresses the lateral dimension of the residential function. The business bid-rent function, steep at small values of lateral distance ρ, flattens as ρ increases. The residential function, though positively sloped at small values of ρ, acquires its generally negative-exponential character as ρ increases. Competitive bidding between the business and residential sectors results in a business district, heavily concentrated around the CBD that tapers out along the radial highway.

In the subcenter case, a positively-sloped avoidance rent segment, extending through an intermediate range of μ, is introduced into the residential function. Competitive bidding results in the development of a business subcenter along the radial highway near the urban limit.

A. THE SIMPLE CASE

The radial dimension of both the business and residential functions take the form of a negative exponential. However, the lateral dimensions of the functions for the two competing sectors take different forms.

Though differences exist among the individual bid-rent functions for the retail, manufacturing, wholesale, and service employment sectors, a negative-exponential function can approximate both the radial and lateral dimensions of these business functions. As a result, the lateral dimension of the business function reaches a maximum value along the radial highway. This occurs because businesses maximize profits, through increased sales and/or decreased transportation costs, by locating close to the highway. Therefore, businesses submit the highest bid for property along highway frontage. But, residential users submit a maximum bid at ρ', a short distance from the highway.

Secondly, business faces a distance-elastic premium rent R_{BP} directly related to the amenities offered by the frontage property such that premium rent decreases with lateral distance from the highway. Businesses seek locations close to the highway in order to minimize transportation costs and maximize visibility. Furthermore, the retail sector and to a lesser extent the service sector submit higher bids for frontage locations.

Primarily, the lateral dimension of the business bid-rent function develops on the normal rent function R_{BN} which decreases for increasing values of ρ due to increasing transportation costs such that normal rent also decreases with lateral distance with the exception that

$$(1) \quad \delta R_{BP} / \delta \rho < \delta R_{BN} / \delta \rho$$

The result is a function with an upper envelope. This envelope function, very steep at small values of ρ, quickly flattens for increasing values of ρ such that a negative-exponential function[7] can approximate the envelope function as

$$(2) \quad R_B (\mu, \rho) = R_B (\mu, 0) e^{-\zeta \rho}$$

Where

$$(3) \quad R_B (\mu, 0) = R_B (0, 0) e^{-\gamma \mu}$$

in which ζ is greater than or equal to γ and R_B is inversely related to both ρ and μ.

---

[7] Mills |65| and McDonald and Bowman |62| offer empirical evidence that the negative exponential function serves as a good approximation of the business bid-rent function.

(4) $R_B(\mu, \rho) / \delta\rho < 0 \quad = R_B(\mu, \rho) / \delta\mu < 0$

The radial dimension of the residential function develops similar to the radial business function. However, the lateral dimension of the residential bid-rent function develops as a two-fold procedure. Residential disamenities, though high at $\rho = 0$, decline through increasing values of ρ. In the case of residential land, high levels of air and noise pollution and low levels of security produce a high level of disamenities that continue for a greater distance ρ than they would for the agricultural sector. As a result, a residential disamenity refund function R_{RD} approximates the residential bidders behavior such that

(5) $R_{RD}(\mu, \rho) = R_{RD}(\mu, 0) \, e^{-\beta\rho}$

for which R_{RD} is directly related to the level of disamenities which is inversely related to ρ. This means that the first and second order partial derivatives of R_{RD} in respect to ρ are negative and positive, respectively. A negative exponential function also approximates the normal portion of the lateral residential bid R_{RN}. Due to commuting costs, residential bid-rent decreases as ρ increases. The resulting lateral dimension of the residential function increases for $0 < \rho < \rho'$, reaches a maximum at ρ', and decreases for $\rho > \rho'$. Therefore, the entire residential bid-rent function takes the form of

$$(6) \quad R_R(\mu, \rho) = R_{RN}(0, 0)\, e^{-(\psi\mu + \tau\rho)} - R_{RD}(0, 0)\, e^{-(\gamma\mu + \beta\rho)}$$

in which R_{RN} is greater than R_{RD}, R_R is greater than the constant minimum rent beyond the urban boundary **R** *bar*, and β is greater than or equal to τ for which the first and second order conditions in respect to ρ are

$$(7) \quad \delta R_R(\mu, \rho) / \delta\rho = -\tau R_{RN}(\mu, 0)\, e^{-\tau\rho} + \beta R_{RD}(\mu, 0)\, e^{-\beta\rho}$$

which equals 0 at ρ' and

$$(8) \quad \delta^2 R_R(\mu, \rho) / \delta\rho^2 = \tau^2 R_{RN}(\mu, 0)\, e^{-\tau\rho} - \beta^2 R_{RD}(\mu, 0)\, e^{-\beta\rho}$$

At increasing values of μ, the lateral business bid dominates the residential bid for a short distance on either side of the highway.[8]

---

[8] The reader is referred to Goodman [33] for a similar exposition done in respect to radial distance.

However, the residential bid dominates thereafter (fig. 7). The equilibrium points $\rho^*(\mu)$ are the lateral locations that satisfy the condition that R_B equals R_R.

(9) $R_B(\mu, \rho^*(\mu)) = R_R(\mu, \rho^*(\mu))$

Therefore, the total rent received by landlords at distance μ is which in functional form is

$$(10) \quad R = 2[\int_{0}^{\rho^*(\mu)} R_B(\mu, \rho)\, \delta\rho + \int_{\rho^*(\mu)}^{\rho_M(\mu)} R_R(\mu, \rho)\, \delta\rho]$$

under the conditions that

$$0 < \rho < \rho^*(u) \qquad \qquad \rho^*(u) < \rho < \rho_M(u)$$
$$============= \qquad \qquad ================$$
$$R_B > R_R \qquad\qquad\qquad R_R > R_B$$

which means that businesses outbid households (if unencumbered by zoning restrictions) for all urban land to a distance $\rho^*(\mu)$

from the highway. All urban land beyond $\rho^*(\mu)$ goes to residential users.[9] Measurement extends to $\rho_M(\mu)$, the mid-line between any two radial highways.

The residential bid reflects levels of neighborhood amenities. Residential neighborhood amenities are natural or artificial pleasantries such as lakes, woods, quality schools, low taxes or good public security that increase the perceived value of residential locations in that neighborhood and thus result in an increased residential bid. Businesses, however, may view these same pleasantries with indifference or disdain. At certain values of μ, a sufficiently high level of residential neighborhood amenities may result in dominance of the residential bid at all values of ρ. However at other values of μ, sufficiently low neighborhood amenities may result in business bid dominance at all values of ρ.

---

[9] There are exceptions to this rule, such as the case in which an urban area expands to encompass an existing business site. The amount of disamenities produced by the business may be sufficient to discourage conversion of adjacent land to residential use. Grether and Mieszkowski |36| present a more extensive discussion of proximity effects.

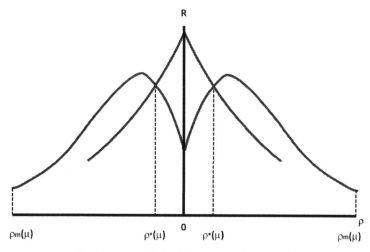

**Fig. 7. Competition Between Business and
Residential Users**

For both functions, the radial dimension expresses as a negative exponential. On the average, one can expect the radial dimension of the business bid-rent function R_B to be steeper than the radial dimension of the residential bid-rent function R_R. Though the values of the radial gradients may vary from the average values in respect to both functions, one can expect the business function to be steeper than the residential function along the mid-line between the radial highways. However, according to the empirical work on business and residential gradients done by Mills [65] and MaCauley [54], one can expect business rents to decline at a lesser rate than residential rents, along the radial highway. The relationship between the business and residential bid-rent topography changes at incremental distances from the CBD. This change measures as a decreasing value of $\rho^*(\mu)$, proven by iteration using increasing values of μ.[10] As the values of μ increase with distance from the CBD, the arc of the wedge (defined as twice the value of ρ) also increases. The business bid-rent surface dominates at all values of ρ during the initial stage of progression. However, due to changes in the rates of decrease of the two bid-rent topographies at greater values of μ and ρ, the domination of the business bid recedes, leaving an increasing percentage of land to residential use such that

(12) $\quad \delta(\, \rho_M(\mu) - \rho^*(\mu)\,)\,/\,\delta\mu > 0$

And

(13) $\quad \delta[\,(\,\rho_M(\mu) - \rho^*(\mu))\,/\,\rho(\mu)\,]\,/\,\delta\mu > 0$

These relative changes in topography result in a business zone in the shape of a spear tip. This zone concentrates around the

---

[10] A simplified demonstration of the decreasing value of $\varrho'(u)$ as u increases can be performed using the following parameters: $R_R(0,0) = .6R_B(0,0)$; $\gamma = .1$; $\zeta = .1$; $\psi = .05$; $\tau = .05$; and $\beta = .1$.

CBD and tapers asymptotically outward along the radial highway (fig. 8). In this case, one estimates the total rent received by the landlords with the double integral

$$(14) \quad R = 2 \left[\int_0^{\bar{\mu}} \int_0^{\rho^*(\mu)} R_B(0, 0) e^{-(\gamma\mu + \zeta\rho)} \, \delta\rho \, \delta\mu \right.$$

$$+ \int_0^{\bar{\mu}} \int_{\rho^*(\mu)}^{\rho_M(\mu)} (R_{RN}(\mu, 0) e^{-\tau\rho}$$

$$\left. - R_{RD}(\mu, 0) e^{-\beta\rho}) \, \delta\rho \, \delta\mu \right]$$

in which

$$(15) \quad R_B(\mu, 0) = R_B(0, 0) e^{-\gamma\mu}$$

and

$$(16) \quad R_R(\mu, 0) = R_{RN}(0, 0) e^{-(\psi\mu + \tau\rho)}$$
$$- R_{RD}(0, 0) e^{-(\gamma\mu + \beta\rho)}$$

evaluated at ρ equals 0.

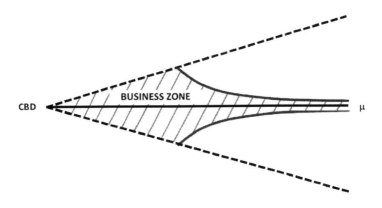

Fig. 8. Tapering Business Zone Near CBD

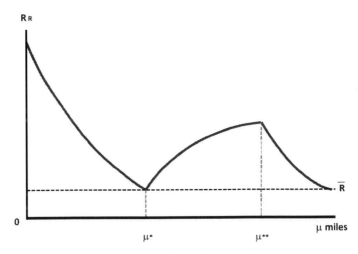

Fig. 9. Introduction of a Positive Rent Segment

B. THE SUBCENTER CASE: INITIAL RESULTS FROM COMPETITIVE BIDDING

Initially the radial dimension of the residential bid takes the form of a negative exponential. However, if one alters the radial dimension of the residential bid-rent function, the land-use pattern produced by competitive bidding differs substantially from the previous case. The introduction of a positively-sloped avoidance rent segment (fig. 9) into the radial dimension of the residential function results in the development a business subcenter close to the urban limit μ *bar*. This altered residential bid-rent function which draws on the work of Goodman [32], Richardson [85], and McDonald and Bowman [63], has the characteristics of

$$(17) \quad \delta R_R(\mu, \rho) / \delta\mu \ < 0$$

$$\delta^2 R_R(\mu, \rho) / \delta\mu^2 > 0$$

for $0 < \mu < \mu^*$

$$(18) \quad \delta R_R (\mu, \rho) / \delta\mu \; > 0$$

$$\delta^2 R_R (\mu, \rho) / \delta\mu^2 < 0$$

for $\mu^* < \mu < \mu^{**}$ and

$$(19) \quad \delta R_R (\mu, \rho) / \delta\mu \; < 0$$

$$\delta^2 R_R (\mu, \rho) / \delta\mu^2 > 0$$

for $\mu^{**} < \mu < \mu$ *bar* such that

$$(20) \quad R_R (0, 0) > R_R (\mu^{**}, \rho) > R_R (\mu^*, \rho)$$

The avoidance-rent segment results from a relatively high level of residential neighborhood amenities at outlying distances from the CBD. For outlying locations, a perceived or real quality difference in residential location decision variables such as schools, taxes, public safety, pollution, congestion, and/or cultural homogeneity has resulted in higher residential bids.[11]

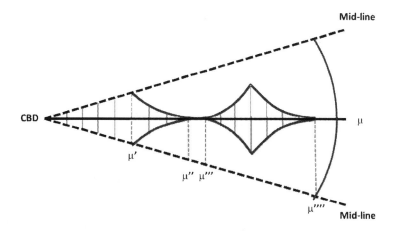

Fig. 10. Business Center and Subcenter

---

[11] The reader is directed to Follain and Malpezzi [23], Mayer [55], Segelhorst and Brady [90], and White [103] for discussions of the location decision variables, in context of suburbanization, which have resulted in avoidance-bid rents.

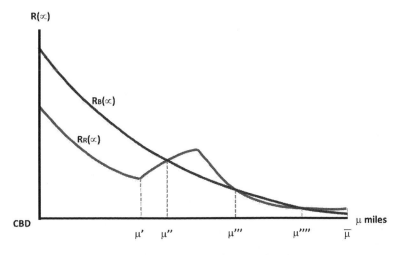

Fig. 11. Bid Rents along the Radial Highway

Business and residential bid-rents alternate in dominance at incremental distances μ from the CBD. An iterative process using increasing values of μ to solve for values of $\rho^*(\mu)$ indicates that $\rho^*(\mu)$ increases and decreases twice. Initially, the business bid-rent surface dominates at all values of ρ. As the residential function enters its avoidance rent phase, bidding allocates land between business and residential users such that the residential bid dominates for land from $\rho^*(\mu)$ through $\rho_M(\mu)$. The comparative statics reiterate those of the previous case. As μ increases however, the residential bid dominates at all values of ρ.

The residential bid-rent function re-enters a negative exponential phase after reaching a local maximum at μ^{**}. Then the business bid-rent topography re-emerges at μ''' to continue as the dominant bid along the highway towards μ'''' (fig. 10 and 11). From μ''' through μ'''', both the absolute and relative quantities of business land initially increase such that $\rho^*(\mu)$ is directly related to μ and

$$(21) \quad \delta[\,(\rho^*(\mu))\,/\,\rho_M(\mu)\,]\,/\,\delta\mu > 0$$

Thereafter, these quantities decrease such that $\rho^*(\mu)$ is inversely related to μ and

$$(22) \quad \delta[\,(\rho^*(\mu))\,/\,\rho_M(\mu)\,]\,/\,\delta\mu < 0$$

Therefore, competitive bidding results in the development of a business subcenter.

Two business zones exist in each radial segment. A diamond-shaped zone extends outward from the CBD. After reaching a maximum width at distance μ', it converges toward the highway and ends at μ''. The second business zone emerges at μ''' and takes a form similar to the first zone. As a result, a double integral serves to estimate the total rent received by the landlord from business and residential users in a radial segment such that

$$(23) \quad R = 2[\int_0^{\bar{\mu}} \int_0^{\rho*(\mu)} R_B (0, 0) e^{-(\gamma\mu + \zeta\rho)} \delta\rho \, \delta\mu$$

$$+ \int_0^{\bar{\mu}} \int_{\rho*(\mu)}^{\rho_M(\mu)} (R_{RN} (\mu, 0) e^{-\tau\rho}$$

$$- R_{RD} (\mu, 0) e^{-\beta\rho}) \, \delta\rho \, \delta\mu]$$

for which

$$(24) \quad R_{RD} (\mu^*, 0) = R_R (0, 0) e^{-\psi\mu^*}$$

and

$$(25) \quad R_R (\mu^{**}, 0) = R_R (\mu^*, 0) + (\mu - \mu^*)^n$$

where **0 < n < 1**, such that

$$(26) \quad R_R(\mu, 0) = R_{RN}(\mu, 0) - R_{RD}(\mu, 0)$$

which functionally is

$$(27) \quad R_R(\mu, 0) = R_R(0, 0)\, e^{-\psi\mu}$$

when $\mu \leq \mu^*$

$$(28) \quad R_R(\mu, 0) = R_R(\mu^*, 0) + (\mu - \mu^*)^n$$

when $\mu^* < \mu \leq \mu^{**}$ and

$$(29) \quad R_R(\mu, 0) = R_R(\mu^{**}, 0)\, e^{-\psi(\mu-\mu^{**})}$$

in which

$$(30) \quad R_R (\mu^{**}, 0) = R_R (\mu^*, 0) + (\mu^{**} - \mu^*)^n$$

when $\mu^{**} < \mu \leq \mu$ *bar* such that $R_R(\mu, 0)$ is equal to **R** *bar*. This means that a change in residential-bid behavior influences the development of business subcenters midway between the CBD and the urban limit.

III. THE PROCESS OF AGGLOMERATION
IN BUSINESS SUBCENTERS
A. INTRODUCTION

Richardson [86] states that any subcenter needs a minimum critical size to create an agglomerative pull. Therefore, only a limited number of subcenters viably challenge the CBD, a challenge reinforced by agglomeration of unlike activities due to locational interdependence.[12]

Urbanization economies result in the primary growth of subcenters. Potential overall economic activity appears greater in the case of population subcentering (avoidance-rent phase) due to

---

[12] The reader is directed to the seminal work of Koopmans and Beckmann [48] and the recent works of Tauchen and Witte [93] and Beckmann and Thisse [6] for a discussion of location of economic activities. For recent discussions of central and non-central agglomeration economies, the reader is directed to the recent works of Braid [8, 9], Fujita [27], Fujita and Rivera-Batiz [28], Pascal and McCall [76], and Rivera-Batiz [87].

increased population density (McDonald, [61]). This provides increased customer and labor market density for the retailing and service sectors and an increased labor market density for the wholesale and manufacturing sectors near the business subcenter (Erickson and Wasylenko [21]).

Adapting Weber's [100] agglomeration model to the present model develops a mechanism for explaining the secondary growth of subcenters. Secondary growth results from increasing localization economies (Nakamura [73]) and increasing internal economies of scale of each subcenter firm. Localization economies result in part from the location decision of other firms and the size of the subcenter such that suboptimal subcenter size will diminish localization economies. Internal economies of scale result in part from urbanization economies which in turn develop from factor market supplies. Primarily, population subcentering increases the local labor market supply which in turn contributes to a localized increase of internal economies of scale.

Competitive bidding between business and residential users has established a subcenter. In the following analysis, businesses bid against one another in an effort to establish themselves on the best vacant subcenter land. Such bidding reflects expected gains in profits from increases in both localization economies and internal economies of scale.

Expected gains vary with site location within the subcenter because firms submit higher bids for more preferred locations. The most preferred location emerges as the center of agglomeration (μ^+, ρ^+) which represents the location that minimizes long-haul transportation costs along the radial and lateral roadways subject to maximizing gains from localization economies and internal economies of scale.

This analysis treats localization economies and internal economies of scale together as agglomeration economies. Increasing agglomeration economies affects both size and shape of the business subcenter and the resulting height and overall shape of the business rent topography[13]. The enlargement of the business subcenter can occur from both radial and lateral expansions around the center of agglomeration (μ^+, ρ^+).

As a result, the distance between the CBD and the inner end of the business subcenter, μ''', may decrease and the distance

---

[13] Topography is defined in this usage as the mapping of the rent surface produced by the combination of lateral and radial bid functions.

between the CBD and the outer end of the subcenter, μ'''', may increase. Furthermore, if the urban limit forms the outer boundary of the subcenter, u may increase. Finally, the lateral limit of the subcenter $\rho^*(\mu)$ may first increase and then decrease throughout the range μ''' to μ''''.

B. THE PROCESS OF AGGLOMERATION IN BUSINESS CENTERS AND SUBCENTERS

In this analysis, firms possess perfect knowledge of all costs, productivity, and potential gains from economies of agglomeration for all firms. All firms, equal in size and perfectly competitive having equal constant pre-agglomeration average cost C, bid for equal-sized plots of land. Agglomeration results in a reduction of average cost such that post-agglomeration average cost $AC(Q)$ reaches a minimum at production level Q_m. Economies of agglomeration $\phi(Q)$ occur as a function of production such that

$$(31) \quad \phi(Q) = C - AC(Q)$$

Therefore, total gains from agglomeration, expressed as $Q\phi(Q)$, reach a maximum at Q^*, the level of production which maximizes total gains from agglomeration (fig. 12). Thus, the small competitive firms combine until the aggregate of firms reaches the level of production Q^*.

The firm initiating the aggregation process chooses a location central to all potential members of the aggregate in order to maximize gains from agglomeration subject to minimizing post-aggregation long-haul transportation costs. Therefore, the initiator locates along or near the highway at an intermediate radial distance within the subcenter. This location emerges as the center of agglomeration (μ^+, ρ^+).

Because of its role and geographic location in the aggregation, the initiator achieves the lowest average cost $AC(q)$ of all the aggregated firms. Therefore, the initiator emerges as the most profitable division in the aggregate. This division optimizes its own output q subject to the optimal output of the aggregate Q^* such that the initiator's individual gain from agglomeration, expressed as $q\phi(Q)$, reaches a maximum at q^*, the level of output which maximizes divisional gains from agglomeration.

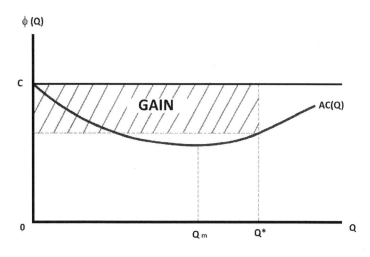

Fig. 12. Total Gains From Agglomeration

The landlords absorb the gains from agglomeration by all firms (divisions) as an addition to Ricardian rent. As a result, the firm (division) located at the center of agglomeration pays the highest rent premium $P_G(\mu^+, \rho^+)$.

Firms (divisions) occupying the plots in the first ring around the center of agglomeration pay the next highest premium. Gains from agglomeration diminish with distance from the center of agglomeration such that the total Premium of Agglomeration received by the landlord equals

$$(32) \qquad P_G = 2[\int_{\mu'''}^{\mu''''} \int_{0}^{\rho*(\mu)} P_G(\mu^+, \rho^+) e^{-(c|\mu - \mu^+| + \tau\rho)} \, \delta\rho \, \delta\mu]$$

Total pre-agglomeration rent received by the landlord from the subcenter equals

$$(33) \qquad R_B = 2[\int_{\mu'''}^{\mu''''} \int_{0}^{\rho*(\mu)} R_B(0, 0) e^{-(\gamma\mu + \zeta\rho)} \, \delta\rho \, \delta\mu]$$

such that the total rent received equals

$$(34) \qquad R_{BG} = 2[\int_{\mu'''}^{\mu''''} \int_{0}^{\rho*(\mu)} (P_G(\mu^+, \rho^+) e^{-(c|\mu - \mu^+| + \tau\rho)}$$

$$+ R_B(0, 0) e^{-(\alpha\mu + \zeta\rho)}) \delta\rho \, \delta\mu]$$

If P_G is greater than zero at all values of μ and ρ in the subcenter, μ''' decreases in value while μ'''' and $\rho^*(\mu)$ increase in value as businesses outbid residential users for land adjacent to the periphery of the original subcenter. Therefore, the introduction of agglomeration economies results in expansion of the business subcenter.

Furthermore, sufficiently large gains from agglomeration and the resulting Premium of Agglomeration P_G at the center of agglomeration (μ^+, ρ^+) locally maximizes the business bid-rent in the subcenter at the center of agglomeration (Bender and Hwang [7] and Grimaud [37]). This concurs with the findings of White [102].

V. NOTES ON THE RETAIL TRADE SECTOR

The case of the Retail Trade closely follows the scenario just presented. The next chapter further explores this case in an empirical study of Major Retail Centers (MRCs) in ten SMSAs. There exists empirical evidence that the lateral position of the center of agglomeration in MRCs moves away from the position $(\mu^+, 0)$ (along the radial highway frontage at the CBD) as the distance between the MRCs and the CBD increases. As a result, outlying MRCs tend to have their center of agglomeration situated at $(\mu^+, \rho^+(\mu))$ some distance from the highway such that $\rho^+(\mu)$ increases with radial distance from the CBD.

It appears that this off-centering results from the changing profile of retailing in its suburbanization over time. In older central-city shopping areas, retailers bid the greatest premium rent for sidewalk frontage along Main Street. Conversely, retailers bid less for above ground floor locations along Main Street (Friedrichs and Goodman [25, 26]) and for locations along side streets.

However as Retail Trade has suburbanized, it has shown the propensity to concentrate in shopping plazas, malls, and mega-malls which have centers of agglomeration at increasing distances from the highway, respectively. In an enclosed mall, for example, the center of the main corridor forms the center of agglomeration. An upscale major department store, located near the center of the corridor, generally serves as the hub of the mall. Midscale retailers serve as anchors at either end of the main corridor. Expansive parking lots surround the enclosed mall.

In contrast, retailers having high size-to-cost ratio products (such as furniture) locate around the periphery of the mall property. Profitability for the peripheral stores depends more on low-cost floor space than on agglomeration economies.

As a result of the changing profile of retailing, the Premium of Agglomeration takes the form of equation 32 in the preceding section. This implies that retailing reaches peak activity in outlying MRC at a radial distance μ^+ and a lateral distance $\rho^+(\mu)$ either side of the highway. Chapter 4 further explores this issue.

VI. SUMMARY AND SUGGESTIONS
FOR FURTHER RESEARCH

In this chapter, I have developed an extended monocentric model. This general model contains a large but finite number of concentric circular streets around the CBD and a small number of equidistant highways radiating from the CBD. As a result, the general model takes the shape of a multi-pointed star. More specifically, I have developed a land-bidding model in one uniform segment of the general monocentric urban model.

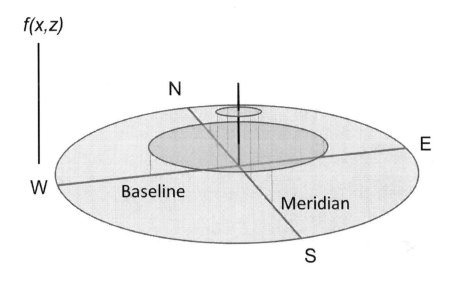

12.B SETUP OF GENERAL MONOCENTRIC MODEL

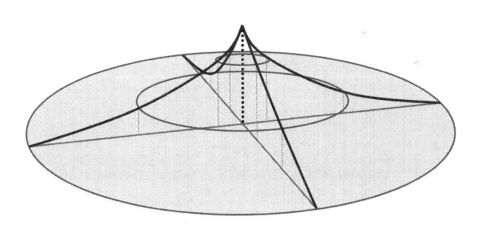

12.C GENERAL MONOCENTRIC MODEL

The specific model analyzes competitive bidding among business and residential urban land users. The existence of a small number of radial highways has resulted in business-bid dominance for highway frontage. In addition, competitive bidding between business and residential users has resulted in the development of a business center in the first case and both a business center and subcenter in the second case which introduces an avoidance-rent segment into the residential bid-rent function. Furthermore, agglomeration economies have resulted in the augmentation of the business subcenter.

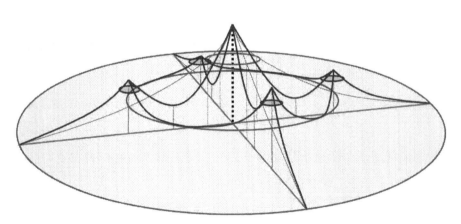

12.D MODEL WITH ONE SUBCENTER RING

The model outlined above offers numerous possibilities for further research. Initially, the process of subcenter formation and agglomeration suggests further exploration in respect to open and closed cities (previous research by Wheaton [101]) and the predominance of any of the four employment sectors (previous research by Mills [65], MaCauley [54]). Secondly, one could analyze changes in $\rho^*(\mu)$ which forms the boundary between business and residential urban land using iterative techniques for a wide range of bid-rent gradient values (previous research by Mills [65], Moses and Williamson [72], and MaCauley [54] has indicated that these values change significantly over time and vary with city size).

These resulting values of $\rho^*(\mu)$ would enable total integration of the total rent equations. Thirdly, one could perform empirical tests of the specific lateral and avoidance bid-rent functions which contribute to the uniqueness of the preceding model for a number of actual urban areas that have developed along a system of radial highways.

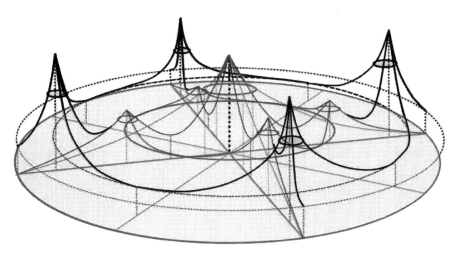

12.E MODEL WITH DOMINANT SECOND SUBCENTER RING

$$(42) \quad \eta_1 = (\ \delta D(\mu_1) \ / \ \delta(\mu_1))\ (\mu^{**}/2)$$

Further, the coefficients in column eight multiplied by $(\mu\ \textit{bar}\ -$ $\mu^{**})/2$ produce the elasticities in column 10 such that

$$(43) \quad \eta_2 = (\ \delta D(\mu_2) \ / \ \delta(\mu_2))\ ((\bar{\mu} - \mu^{**})/2)$$

As μ^{**} and $(\mu\ \textit{bar}\ -\ \mu^{**})$ decrease in size, the two elasticities converge towards 0.

The coefficients in column seven multiplied by μ^{**} are added to the natural log of densities at the CBD in column five to produce the natural log of peak densities at μ^{**} in column six. The anti-logs of densities in columns five and six appear as employment-per-square-mile and sales-per-square-mile in columns three and four.

In all cases that produce results, peak activity occurs some distance away from the central business district (column 2). Furthermore with the exception of Chicago which has a peak close to the CBD, the SMSAs appear to have peak densities midway between the CBD and the furthest MRC. In accordance with the model, peak subcenter density is greater than CBD density. For example, the least employment-density increase occurs in Denver while the greatest occurs in Indianapolis which suggests that retailing has suburbanized the least and the most in those cities. Though there is no clear pattern of the peak to CBD relationship, it does appear on average that densities increase by a factor of two to three.

ORIENTATION

PHOTOS AND MAPS

OF

THE TEN SMSAs

ATLANTA CBD

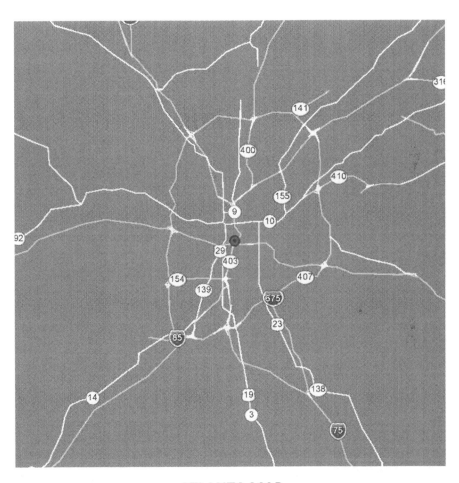

ATLANTA MAP

BALTIMORE CBD

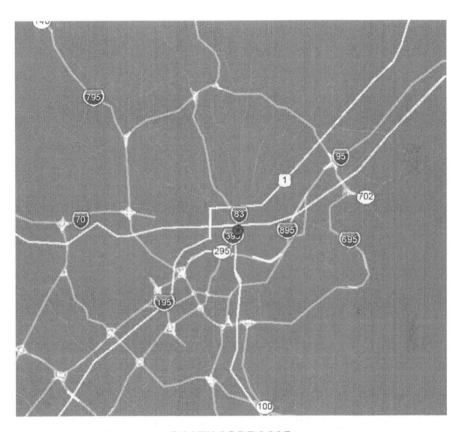

BALTIMORE MAP

CHICAGO CBD

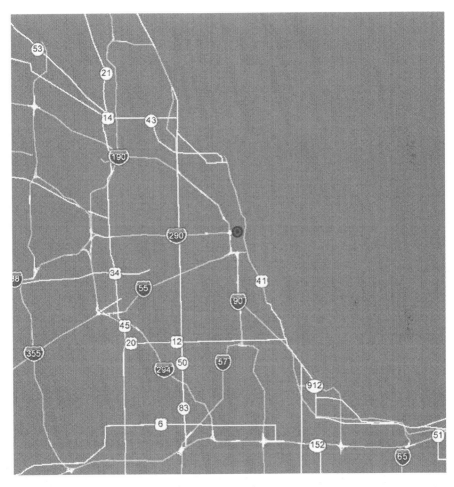

CHICAGO MAP

DENVER CBD

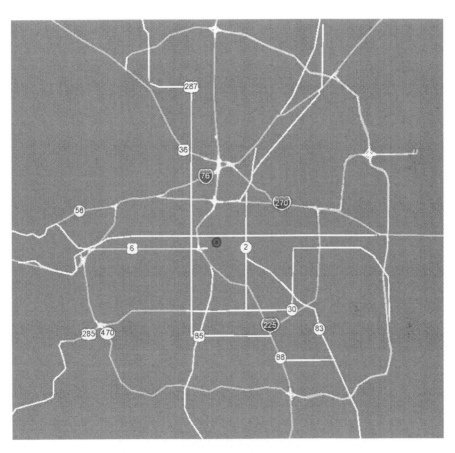

DENVER MAP

DETROIT CBD

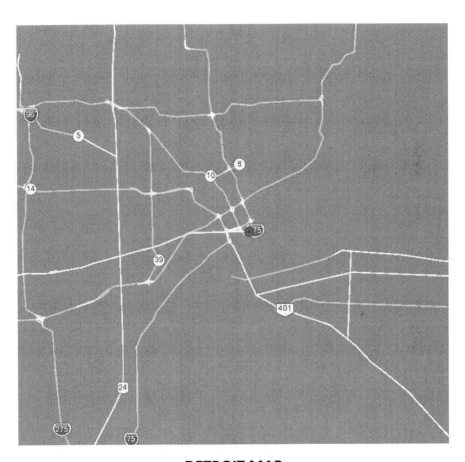

DETROIT MAP

HOUSTON CBD

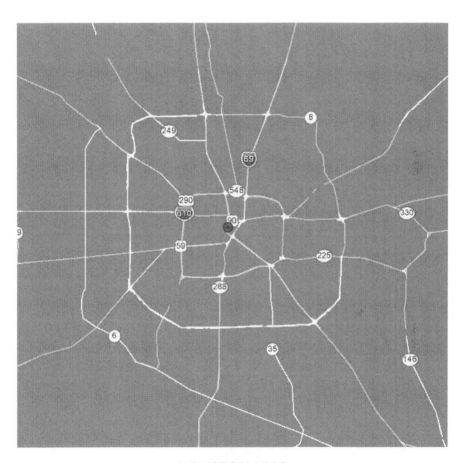

HOUSTON MAP

INDIANAPOLIS CBD

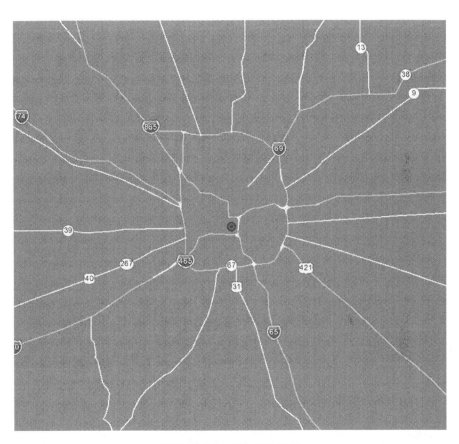

INDIANAPOLIS MAP

PHILADELPHIA CBD

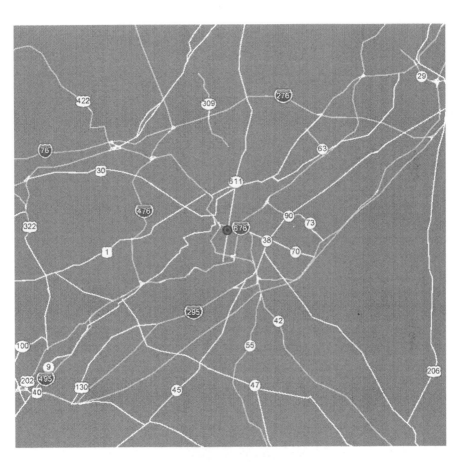

PHILADELPHIA MAP

PITTSBURGH CBD

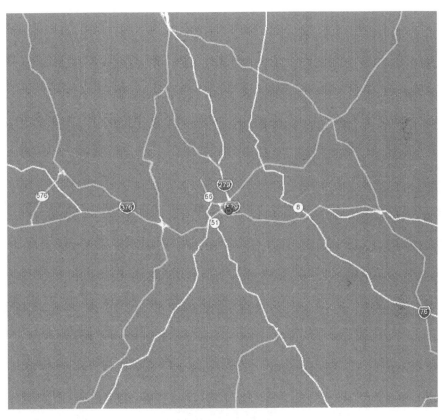

PITTSBURGH MAP

WASHINGTON CBD

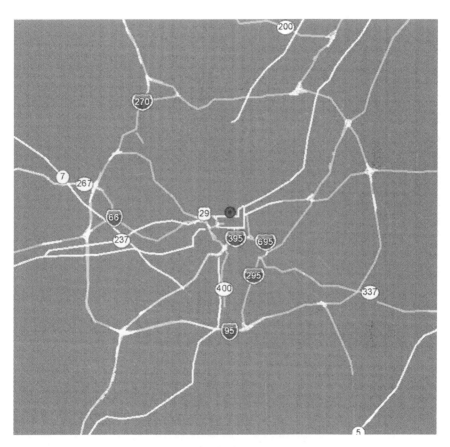

WASHINGTON MAP

CHAPTER 4

I. INTRODUCTION

A. GENERAL BACKGROUND

This study estimates and ascertains the existence and location of peak activity in business subcenters. To achieve this goal, the current study uses a two-step method. This method proves optimal because the heteroskedastic nature of much of the data and lack of exogenous local extrema present problems in finding significant model specifications.

Given data for 295 Major Retail Centers from ten SMSAs, this study uses a comparative t-test and a Davidson-MacKinnon model-specification error test (J-test) to ascertain the existence and location of peak activity in retail subcenters for the separate SMSAs. This study executes these tests alternately for employment density and gross sales density functions. It follows from the model and hypothesis developed in sections II and III of this chapter, that one peak of employment/business subcenter activity should exist at distance μ^{**} miles from the Central Business District (CBD). Furthermore, peak subcenter activity may exist at a short lateral distance ρ^{**} miles from a radial highway. Distances μ^{**} and ρ^{**} also suggest the location of the center of agglomeration μ^{+} and ρ^{+} discussed in Section III of Chapter 3. Therefore in both the employment and gross sales density functions, evidence of radial and lateral locations of peak activity should appear as local radial and lateral maxima. The radial maxima are determined directly. However, due to relatively small sample sizes, the existence of lateral maxima is inferred by the sign of the lateral gradients.

The usual procedure for density estimation employs a piece-wise linear or polynomial regressions. This proves relatively simple if there exist exogenous local extrema (Dubin and Sung [19], and Suits, Mason and Chan [92]). However when the need exists to estimate these extrema endogenously, greater problems of model-specification error arise. Furthermore, with the highly heteroskedastic data for some SMSAs of the current study, these model specification tests prove spurious due to a shortage of significant competing specifications on which to base the tests. However, it remains possible to endogenously estimate and ascertain the location of local maxima through alternate methods. Therefore, procedures such as the J-test for model-specification error provide a superior means for selecting the better of two competing models by inspecting pairs of t-ratios.

This study employs the J-test as part of the two-step method outlined above. First, the study develops a set of competing model specifications that helps approximate the general locations of local maxima. Second, the most plausible of the competing specifications enter into a final round of model-specification error testing. In this round, a J-test procedure tests pairs of competing model specifications to determine the specification that provides the best estimate of the local maximum in each SMSA studied.

B. THE PROBLEM

The problem addressed in this study surfaces by fitting the expanded standard urban model (equation 35) to data for ten radial monocentric SMSAs. The results for employment density in Table 1 indicate that the traditional expectation of a negative radial gradient only holds for five of the ten SMSAs studied when unconstrained Ordinary Least Squares is applied. When the intercept is constrained to the density at the CBD, only four of the ten have negative gradients. Furthermore, the lateral gradients vary between positive and negative in the same number of instances. The situation improves slightly in the unconstrained results for sales density as seven of the ten SMSAs have negative radial gradients (Table 2). But, this number declines to 1 when the intercept is constrained to CBD density. With the introduction of the constraint, the number of SMSAs having negative lateral gradients declines from 5 to 3. In addition, both the positive and negative gradients are usually much steeper but worse fitting than their respective radial gradients.

C. THE SOLUTION

To reiterate, the aforementioned results suggest in a majority of cases that 1. Retail densities increase with radial distance, or 2. Activity peaks at a subcenter location. The current study addresses the problem from the standpoint of the second premise and develops a model with two radial phases.

TABLE 1. EMPLOYMENT DENSITY					
SMSA		UNCONSTRAINED		CONSTRAINED	
	ln D(0)	GAMMA	ZETA	GAMMA	ZETA
ATLANTA	8.5358	.01590	.15032	.06441	.17128
		(.401)	(.718)	(3.824)	(.821)
BALTIMORE	9.1588	-.02937	.36329	-.01036	.38980
		(-.952)	(.862)	(-.580)	(.928)
CHICAGO	9.493	-.03215	-.13551	-.01292	-.01539
		(-5.131)	(-2.095)	(-3.661)	(-.275)
DENVER	8.8529	-.08254	.19112	-.02578	.26199
		(-1.143)	(.918)	(-.948)	(1.374)
DETROIT	8.3001	-.03484	.14694	.02760	.06768
		(-1.659)	(1.353)	(2.763)	(.638)
HOUSTON	8.2189	.00551	-.13854	.08377	.16912
		(.258)	(-1.049)	(9.467)	(1.567)
INDIANAPOLIS	6.9927	.02277	-.51532	.30040	-.71366
		(.344)	(-1.278)	(12.422)	(-1.780)
PHILADELPHIA	9.2162	.01575	-.03228	.33098	-.17011
		(1.039)	(-.112)	(.313)	(-.650)
PITTSBURGH	9.8863	.03567	-.54919	-.00567	-.83688
		(1.909)	(-1.484)	(-.527)	(-2.360)
WASHINGTON	8.9829	-.04074	.12902	.02908	.10850
		(-2.032)	(.603)	(2.635)	(.507)

TABLE 2. SALES DENSITY					
CITY		UNCONSTRAINED		CONSTRAINED	
	ln D(0)	GAMMA	ZETA	GAMMA	ZETA
ATLANTA	12.2092	.02365	.17272	.10644	.20849
		(.563)	(.780)	(5.975)	(.944)
BALTIMORE	12.9568	-.03702	.15505	.01962	.23405
		(-1.041)	(.319)	(.952)	(.483)
CHICAGO	13.5059	-.03140	-.14454	-.00836	-.00060
		(-4.427)	(-1.974)	(-2.092)	(-.009)
DENVER	12.6141	-.09821	.24010	.02267	.39165
		(-1.321)	(1.122)	(.809)	(1.993)
DETROIT	12.0519	-.03073	.11419	.05664	.00329
		(-1.497)	(1.076)	(5.804)	(.032)
HOUSTON	12.2191	-.01315	-.20387	.09453	.21943
		(-.552)	(-1.380)	(9.550)	(1.818)
INDIANAPOLIS	10.9360	-.04073	-.54051	.33555	-.80931
		(-.646)	(-1.405)	(14.547)	(-2.117)
PHILADELPHIA	13.0500	.01195	-.04564	.02127	.05753
		(.752)	(-.151)	(1.919)	(.209)
PITTSBURGH	13.6191	.02491	-.53630	.00943	-.64403
		(1.373)	(-1.493)	(.903)	(-1.872)
WASHINGTON	12.9380	-.04859	.03618	.04946	.00736
		(-2.239)	(.156)	(4.140)	(.032)

The null hypothesis, H_N, states that either many or no local maxima exist such that a Davidson-MacKinnon model-specification error test cannot identify peaks of subcenter activity. Strict application of the decision rule, in section IV.F, results in rejection of the null hypothesis for four SMSAs in the employment density studies and eight SMSAs in the sales density studies.

These studies employ a two-step method and data for 295 Major Retail Centers (MRCs) drawn from ten monocentric radial SMSAs to ascertain the existence and location of peak retail subcenter activity in each SMSAs. Estimation of peak activity relies on data sets containing variables composed of observations from U.S. Department of the Census, 1982 Census of Retail Trade [95] and information from a series of metropolitan and U.S. Geological Survey Maps [96].

The current analysis employs two econometric techniques using a two-phase negative-exponential model presented in the following section. These techniques alternately use employment density and gross sales density (proxies for rent density) as the dependent variable. First, a comparative t-test helps approximate the maxima identifying peak subcenter activity within each SMSA. For each SMSA, the t-ratios from this first step identify a set of plausible model specifications which in turn provide an additional variable necessary for the model-specification error test. Second, a Davidson-MacKinnon [18] J-test more precisely ascertains the existence and location of peak subcenter activity.

II. THE MODEL

The current analysis estimates and ascertains the existence and location of peak activity (local maxima) in business subcenters. To accomplish this, the current study uses a two-step method for the estimation and ascertainment procedures. Both of the techniques described in section I. uses a model developed from the standard urban model. This current model is a three-dimensional extension of the robust negative-exponential model employed by Mills [65] and others such that

$$(35) \quad D(\mu, \rho) = D_0 \, e^{-(\gamma\mu + \zeta\rho)}$$

where $D(\mu, \rho)$ is density at radial and lateral distances of μ miles and ρ miles respectively, D_0 is density at the CBD, e is Euler's constant, γ is a radial gradient, and ζ is a lateral gradient.

As evidenced by tables 1 and 2, the above model specification against the retail-trade data set produces a variety of both positive and negative values for γ and ζ. Furthermore, when a simplified model specification of

$$(36) \quad D(\mu) = D_0\, e^{-\gamma\mu}$$

was tried in preliminary studies, a similar variety of positive and negative coefficients appeared. In light of classic studies in the field, this is surprising because this model suggests negative gradients.

In contrast to the traditional works, the present results suggest that activity peaks at a subcenter location. Further, preliminary studies tend to support this assertion and suggest that the distortion results from a model-specification error in the standard negative exponential model.[14]

The standard model is easily re-specified by generalizing the D_0 term. Given that μ^{**} and ρ^{**} represent the radial and lateral

---

[14] Descriptive statistics, data plotting, and histograms indicate density function contours on which multiple peaks occur at locations away from the CBD.

coordinates of the maximum in each SMSA, respectively, $D(\mu^{**}, \rho^{**})$ should replace D_0. Therefore on data samples which evidence a decline on either side of the radial maximum, the current study regresses the altered standard model

$$(37) \quad D(\mu, \rho) = D(\mu^{**}, \rho^{**}) \, e^{-(\gamma\mu + \zeta\rho)}$$

III. THE HYPOTHESES

A maximum in each SMSA identifies the location of peak retail subcenter activity for the employment density and gross sales density functions. It follows from this present study that

1. A maximum exists at one location, and

2. A model-specification error test can accurately identify these locations.

Therefore, the null hypothesis is stated as H_N: Either many or no maximum exist in an SMSA such that a Davidson-MacKinnon model-specification error test (J-test) cannot ascertain the location of peak retail activity.

The alternative hypothesis is stated as

H$_A$: Only one maximum exists in an SMSA such that a Davidson-MacKinnon J-test can ascertain the location of peak retail activity.

IV. ECONOMETRIC METHODS
A. INTRODUCTION

The goal of these studies is to estimate and to ascertain the existence and location of peak subcenter activity. The two-step procedure used here proves sufficient for estimating and ascertaining the location of one peak of subcenter activity occurring at distance μ^{**} from the CBD.

In an earlier study, Dubin and Sung [19] use a spline function to estimate local residential-rent maxima and rent gradients in traditional radial urban segments of one city. This current study parallels theirs in the basic set-up of the radial segments. However, this study concentrates on the retail trade sector for 10 separate SMSAs. Later, Goodman and Dubin [34] work with a Davidson-MacKinnon J-test to compare spatial stratifications in a model of house price determination. The current study follows most directly from that study to develop an estimation technique for the specific study of retail-trade rents as proxied by employment and sales densities.

B. DESCRIPTION OF TECHNIQUES

The current analysis employs two techniques which alternately use employment density and gross-sales density as the dependent variable to ascertain the aforementioned occurrences. The first technique is a comparative t-test. This test applies the model over a continuous series of model specifications. These specifications radially range through each SMSA in one-mile increments. The results provide a set of the best-fitting specifications. If the number of competing plausible specifications for any SMSA is small, the radial location of the maximum identifying peak activity can be approximated with some degree of accuracy. In these cases, the J-test merely ascertains the results of the comparative t-test. However, if there are many competing specifications, then the model-specification error test provides the only recourse to estimate the location of peak activity.

The second technique is the Davidson-MacKinnon J-test. This test places all the plausible specifications into a round of model-specification error testing to estimate the location of peak subcenter activity. The results determine the one good-fitting model specification which has its inflection point at the location of peak activity. Tables 4 and 5 report the results of this two-step test for both employment and sales density for each of the ten SMSAs.

C. COMPARATIVE T-TEST

The comparative t-test serves two purposes. First it produces a vector, β *hat* $_c$, which contains constrained estimates of three coefficients for each plausible model specification. To obtain this vector, the radial measure must be partitioned. In the functional form, μ and ρ of equation 35 become the independent variables **μDRIVML** and **ρDRIVML**. Each specification provides a mark to partition the driving-mile variable **μDRIVML** setting μ^{**} to a specific mile. Once set, **μDRIVML** is divided in to μ_1 and μ_2 by the following method. If **μDRIVML** is less than μ^{**}, μ_1 equals **μDRIVML**. But, if **μDRIVML** is greater than or equal to μ^{**}, μ_1 equals μ^{**}. Similarly, if **μDRIVML** is less than μ^{**}, μ_2 equals **0**. But, if **μDRIVML** is greater than or equal to μ^{**}, μ_2 equals **μDRIVML** minus μ^{**}. In addition to μ_1, μ_2, and **ρDRIVML**, the functional form of the model includes the right-hand constant **ONE**. **ONE** is constrained to either the employment or the sales density at the CBD. Second, the results provide $_c$ which in turn generates the independent-variable vector. The variable y constitutes an additional variable used in each model specification employed in the Davidson-MacKinnon J-test.

D. THE MODEL-SPECIFICATION ERROR TEST

The analysis in this work uses a Davidson-MacKinnon J-test to estimate and ascertain the location of a maximum for each SMSA. The location of this maximum determines the most appropriate specification of the two-phase negative-exponential model. Davidson and MacKinnon [18] primarily draw on the Cox [16] principle of executing a model-specification test on pairs of non-nested hypotheses. In their recent development of a model-specification error test (called a J-test), Davidson and MacKinnon build upon the work of Cox [16], which in turn draws on the more basic works of Hotelling, Hoel, A.D. Roy, and Quandt [40, 39, 88, 83]. From this, Davidson and MacKinnon develop a test for pairs of non-nested hypotheses.

The case of non-nested hypotheses centers on a data set and a pair of alternative hypotheses that are, by assumption, non-nested and thus unranked as to generality. Given that **X** (consisting of **ONE**, μ_{01}, μ_{02}, and **ρDRIVML**) and **Z** (consisting of **ONE**, u_{11}, u_{12}, and **ρDRIVML**) are matrices of independent variables for hypotheses **H$_0$** and **H$_1$**, respectively, the matrices **X** and **Z** are not nested within each other (one cannot obtain all rows or columns of **X** from those of **Z** and vice versa) (Pesaran [77]). Essentially, tests of separate (non-nested) models are specification tests using information about a specific alternative (McAleer [56]).

One can separate these models, expressed as the pair of non-nested hypotheses H_0 and H_1, on the basis of 1. Functional Form, 2. Explanatory Variables, or 3. Sample Stratification. In this study, explanatory variables provide the basis for separating the non-nested hypotheses.

E. THE T-RATIO AS THE SATISFACTORY STATISTIC

The t-ratio serves as the satisfactory test statistic for λ in linear models. Therefore, converting equation 35 and corresponding data into log-linear form accommodates the regression of the functions. Davidson and MacKinnon recommend the J-test when H_0 is linear because linearity makes the J-test extremely easy to use. In the linear case, one merely runs one extra linear regression to test it. The only relevant test statistic for the J-test in the linear case is the t-ratio associated with the estimate of λ [18]. Fisher and McAleer [22] further emphasize that while the estimate of λ itself proves of no importance when testing for H_0 when prior information is available, its t-ratio is a satisfactory statistic for testing H_0.

F. THE DECISION RULE

One model stands as the null only temporarily in testing separate models against one another. A test of the null, H_0, against a single alternative, H_1, is a paired separate test. For this test, four possible outcomes exist: 1. H_0 is significant and H_1 is not; 2. H_1 is significant and H_0 is not; 3. both hypotheses are significant; or 4. both are not. One should reject H_0 in favor of H_1 if the test statistic λ proves significant when H_0 is the null, and λ proves insignificant when H_1 is the null. However, one should reject both models if both λ's prove significant. Finally, the test remains inconclusive if both λ's prove insignificant (Goodman and Dubin [34]).

G.   A CAVEAT ON POTENTIAL SMALL
SAMPLE PROBLEMS

The samples for most of the SMSAs studied are small. Estimates of the resulting coefficients may prove inaccurate due to sample size. In respect to small samples, Davidson and MacKinnon compare the J-test to a number of similar tests and find it difficult to conclude that one test proves more powerful than another and that the performance of all tests appears quite similar in small samples. However in an additional caveat on small samples, Dubin and Goodman [35] have found that sample size can prove important to the results of the J-test.

V. THE FUNCTION

Because of the heteroskedasticity of the data, piece-wise studies suggest that the actual best-fitting continuous function may be a quadratic. However to estimate the local maxima, a two-phase negative-exponential model can serve as a best local estimator and a basis for the J-test in each case. As discussed in the previous section, the t-ratio provides an adequate test statistic for the J-test in linear cases. Therefore in this study, the negative exponential model (equation 35) assumes the log-linear form

$$(38) \quad \ln D(\mu, \rho) = \ln D(0, 0) + \gamma_1 \mu_1 + \gamma_2 \mu_2 + \zeta \rho$$

The resulting functional form of this transformation appears as

$$(39) \quad \ln D(\mu, \rho) = \beta_0 \, \text{ONE} + \beta_1 \mu_1 + \beta_2 \mu_2 + \beta_4 \rho \, \text{DRIVML} + \varepsilon$$

in which **ONE** is a constant whose coefficient β_0 is constrained to **D(0,0)**, the density at the CBD.

μ_1 and μ_2 are partitions (as described in IV.C) of μ**DRIVML** representing radial driving miles from the CBD.

ρ**DRIVML** represents lateral driving miles from the nearest radial highway.

Two densities alternately serve as the dependent variable. These are

1. **Employment Density** - calculated as the number of employees per square mile. (Greater economic activity requires employing more personnel.)

2. **Sales Density** - calculated as dollar sales per square mile. (A greater dollar amount of sales directly reflects a greater amount of economic activity.)

The model-specification error test requires the addition of another independent variable, y *hat* $_1$. y *hat* $_1$ estimates $D(\mu, \rho) =$ Z_i β*bar* $_1$ such that β*bar* $_1$ is an l-vector of estimated coefficients and Z_i is the vector of the original four (including **ONE**) independent variables. Of these four, the μ**DRIVML** specification associated with H_1 which determines the partitioning of μ_1 and μ_2 does not equal that of the μ**DRIVML** specification associated with H_0.

The test regresses y *bar* 1 which is the constrained estimate associated with H_1. The resulting function for testing the null hypothesis H_0 against the alternative hypothesis H_1 takes the form

$$(40) \quad \ln D(\mu, \rho)_0 = \beta_{00} \text{ ONE} + \beta_{01} \mu_{01} + \beta_{02} \mu_{02} + \beta_{03} \rho \text{ DRIVML} + \beta_{04} \hat{y}_1 + \varepsilon$$

such that y *bar* 1 $= Z_{i1} \beta bar$ 1 with μ**DRIVML** partitioned around μ^{**}_0, the mile specification associated with H_0. Conversely, the function for testing H_1 against H_0 takes the form

$$(41) \quad \ln D(\mu, \rho)_1 = \beta_{10} \text{ ONE} + \beta_{11} \mu_{11} + \beta_{12} \mu_{12} + \beta_{13} \rho \text{ DRIVML} + \beta_{14} \hat{y}_{01} + \varepsilon$$

The resulting t-ratios for β_{04} and β_{14} are compared and the decision rule outlined in section VI.F is applied.

VI. DATA SOURCES AND PREPARATION

The data set is composed of observations for ten SMSAs. Each observation represents an individual Major Retail Center (MRC). In part, these SMSAs are chosen on the basis of number of Major Retail Centers. This study relies on the 1982 census descriptions of Major Retail Centers to provide that criteria for selecting the ten SMSAs which contain a total of 295 observations. The number of MRCs in any one of the selected SMSAs ranges from eighteen to fifty-three.

All of the selected SMSAs best represent the ideal monocentric city presented by Mills [64, 65]. Because of that ideal, many major SMSAs remain absent from the current data set. For example, Dallas-Fort Worth and Norfolk-Portsmouth SMSA are bi-centric, and Los Angeles, Phoenix, San Diego, San Francisco, San Jose, Kansas City, Omaha, and New York City are more grid-like than radial. As a result, the ten SMSAs selected include Denver, Washington D.C., Atlanta, Chicago, Indianapolis, Baltimore, Detroit, Philadelphia, Pittsburgh, and Houston. Of these, Indianapolis and Baltimore most closely resemble the monocentric ideal.

Federal census records and SMSA area maps provide the raw data used to develop the current data set [95, 84, 96]. An opisometer and ruler applied to metropolitan street maps, atlases and U.S. Geological Survey maps provide radial and lateral driving distances from the CBD, and the square mile area measurements of individual MRC. These measurements conform to the location and boundary descriptions provided by the U.S. Department of Census, 1982 Census of Retail Trade.

Together, census and map data generate both the dependent and exogenous variables used in this study. The census data for the number of employees, reported by MRC, and gross sales for stores with employees[15], reported by MRC, each divided by the square mile area of the MRC generates two alternate dependent variables--employment density and gross sales density.

To enable OLS estimation, employment and sales densities have been converted to log-linear form. Even with this linearization, heteroskedasticity and multicollinearity by construction remain a problem in some SMSAs for fitting the functions developed in section V. However, in most cases the model fits well enough through the range which contains the peak to perform the J-tests which identify and/or ascertain these locations.

---

[15] A larger measure which includes proprietary businesses is avoided due to the large number of missing observations.

VII. RESULTS

A. INTRODUCTION OF EXPECTATIONS

This analysis seeks to ascertain the existence and location of one peak of subcenter activity in each SMSA. Results should identify this location as a distance μ^{**} from the CBD. Furthermore, in many cases peak subcenter activity is expected to occur as a maximum at a short lateral distance ρ^{**} from a radial highway. However, ρ^{**} is a function μ^{**}. Preliminary results indicate that there exist too few observations in any SMSA to estimate ρ^{**} in the neighborhood of μ^{**}. But, one preliminary study using a combined data set of all SMSAs did produce evidence for employment density that ρ^{**} is located .10 miles from a radial highway at μ^{**}.

B. THE DECISION RULE REVIEWED

As discussed in section IV.F, one should reject H_0 in favor of H_1, if the test statistic proves significant when H_0 is the null, or if the test statistic proves insignificant when H_1 is the null. This study accepts coefficients as significant at the highest possible level in each individual SMSA case.

C. RESULTS REPORTED

The results vary for the ten SMSAs studied. The results indicate that the two-phase model only fails to fit Philadelphia and Pittsburgh for employment density and only Pittsburgh for sales density. The model fits the remaining SMSAs. However, not all of these pass the J-test which means that the existence and location of one peak cannot be ascertained. Only Atlanta, Houston, Detroit, and Washington, D.C. pass the Davidson-MacKinnon employment-density J-test. In comparison, eight SMSAs pass the sales-density J-test. Passing the J-test (rejecting H_N) affirms the existence and ascertains the location of peak activity in subcenters. The significance level of the test statistics for the various cities passing the test vary widely with the least confidence at a significance level of only .25 and the greatest confidence at levels of .005.

Tables 3 and 4 display estimates of peak employment-activity and sales-activity location, densities, gradients, elasticities, results of the J-test, and other useful information. The columns in each of these tables are inter-related and calculated as follows. The coefficients in column seven multiplied by $\mu^{**}/2$ produce the distance elasticities of demand in column nine such that

$$(42) \quad \eta_1 = (\ \delta D(\mu_1)\ /\ \delta(\mu_1)\ )\ (\mu^{**}/2)$$

Further, the coefficients in column eight multiplied by $(\mu$ bar $- \mu^{**})/2$ produce the elasticities in column 10 such that

$$(43) \quad \eta_2 = (\ \delta D(\mu_2)\ /\ \delta(\mu_2)\ )\ ((\bar{\mu} - \mu^{**})/2)$$

As μ^{**} and $(\mu$ bar $- u^{**})$ decrease in size, the two elasticities converge towards **0**.

The coefficients in column seven multiplied by μ^{**} are added to the natural log of densities at the CBD in column five to produce the natural log of peak densities at μ^{**} in column six. The anti-logs of densities in columns five and six appear as employment-per-square-mile and sales-per-square-mile in columns three and four.

TABLE 3. EMPLOYMENT DENSITY, TWO-PHASE MODEL WITH J-TESTS

	(1) mile	(2) u** %	(3) EMP/MI D(0)	(4) EMP/MI D(u**)	(5) ln D(0)	(6) ln D(u**)	(7) GAMMA 1	(8) GAMMA 2	(9) ZETA	(10) ELSTCTY1	(11) ELSTCTY2	(12) REJECT H?	(13) y MILE	(14) t-RATIOS	(15) D.F.	(16) SIG. LEVEL
CITY	u**		D(0)	D(u**)												
ATLANTA	9	.54	5,094	14,240	8.53582	9.56380	.11422 (4.424)	-.07950 (-1.285)	.17385 (.912)	.51397	-.30846	YES	y8 into 9 / y9 into 8	.608 / *-.720	18	.25
BALTIMORE	6	.29	9,497	10,259	9.15878	9.23594	.01286 (.397)	-.03792 (-1.037)	.35441 (.818)	.03858	-.27302	NO	-	-	12	-
CHICAGO	2	.05	13,266	21,917	9.49299	9.99504	.25103 (3.693)	-.03115 (-5.526)	-.12939 (-2.244)	.25103	-.58360	NO	-	-	44	-
DENVER	5	.35	6,995	7,919	8.85293	8.97703	.02482 (.283)	-.07556 (-.875)	.19561 (.886)	.06205	-.33813	NO	-	-	19	-
DETROIT	21	.63	4,024	8,225	8.30008	9.01492	.03404 (3.283)	-.12984 (-2.035)	.19266 (1.636)	.35742	-.79137	YES	y21 into 22 / y22 into 21	*2.833 / 2.499	31	.005
HOUSTON	13	.54	3,710	17,824	8.21892	9.78828	.12072 (6.994)	-.01853 (-.454)	-.01422 (-.104)	.78468	-.10599	YES	y13 into 14 / y14 into 13	*3.061 / 2.813	20	.005
INDIANAPOLIS	9	.67	1,089	20,151	6.99270	9.91104	.32426 (9.192)	-.01707 (-.091)	-.68424 (-1.356)	1.45917	-.03670	NO	-	-	13	-
PHILADELPHIA	-	-	10,058	-	9.21618	-	-	-	-	-	-	NO	-	-	42	-
PITTSBURGH	-	-	19,659	-	9.88631	-	-	-	-	-	-	NO	-	-	15	-
WASHINGTON	16	.56	7,966	18,924	8.98290	9.84818	.05408 (3.987)	-.13985 (-2.689)	.28089 (1.248)	.43264	-.86777	YES	y16 into 17 / y17 into 16	*2.664 / 2.429	23	.01

TABLE 4. SALES DENSITY, TWO-PHASE MODEL WITH J-TESTS

CITY	(1) u** mile	(2) u** %	(3) SAL/MI D(0) ($000)	(4) SAL/MI D(u**) ($000)	(5) ln D(0)	(6) ln D(u**)	(7) GAMMA 1	(8) GAMMA 2	(9) ZETA	(10) ELSTCTY1	(11) ELSTCTY2	(12) REJECT H?	(13) MILE y	(14) t-RATIOS	(15) D.F.	(16) SIG. LEVEL
ATLANTA	13	.78	200,626	1,191,651	12.2092	13.9909	.13705 (6.522)	-.30208 (-1.857)	.13336 (.621)	.89083	-.56791	YES	y13 into 14 / y14 into 13	*1.358 / 1.098	18	.10
BALTIMORE	7	.34	423,708	689,981	12.9568	13.4444	.06966 (2.319)	-.06622 (-1.549)	.15218 (.312)	.24381	-.44367	YES	y6 into 7 / y7 into 6	.654 / *.857	12	.25
CHICAGO	7	.18	733,733	1,193,416	13.5059	13.9923	.06949 (2.865)	-.03125 (-3.868)	-.12927 (-1.737)	.24322	-.50734	YES	y6 into 7 / y7 into 6	2.634 / *2.955	44	.005
DENVER	11	.79	300,710	423,967	12.6141	12.9574	.03121 (.972)	-.17404 (-.522)	.36401 (1.762)	.17166	-.25671	YES	y10 into 11 / y11 into 10	1.617 / *1.750	19	.05
DETROIT	17	.51	171,425	714,658	12.0519	13.4796	.08398 (7.269)	-.10667 (-2.729)	.14741 (1.367)	.71383	-.86349	YES	y17 into 18 / y18 into 17	*2.895 / 2.602	31	.005
HOUSTON	9	.37	202,623	1,358,117	12.2191	14.1216	.21139 (7.036)	-.03176 (-.986)	-.17972 (-1.150)	.95126	-.24519	YES	y9 into 10 / y10 into 9	*3.059 / 2.597	20	.005
INDIANAPOLIS	6	.45	56,162	1,102,951	10.9360	13.9135	.49625 (13.453)	-.08625 (-1.106)	-.54131 (-1.370)	1.48875	-.31481	YES	y6 into 7 / y7 into 6	*3.850 / 2.466	13	.005
PHILADELPHIA	19	.52	465,143	778,995	13.0501	13.5658	.02714 (1.835)	-.00423 (-.098)	.01938 (.068)	.25783	-.03640	NO	-	-	42	-
PITTSBURGH	-	-	821,675	-	13.6191	-	-	-	-	-	-	NO	-	-	15	-
WASHINGTON	11	.39	415,817	1,357,506	12.9380	14.1212	.10756 (6.155)	-.08214 (-2.646)	.03062 (.131)	.59158	-.71503	YES	y11 into 12 / y12 into 11	*2.971 / 2.748	23	.005

In all cases that produce results, peak activity occurs some distance away from the central business district (column 2). Furthermore with the exception of Chicago which has a peak close to the CBD, the SMSAs appear to have peak densities midway between the CBD and the furthest MRC. In accordance with the model, peak subcenter density is greater than CBD density. For example, the least employment-density increase occurs in Denver while the greatest occurs in Indianapolis which suggests that retailing has suburbanized the least and the most in those cities. Though there is no clear pattern of the peak to CBD relationship, it does appear on average that densities increase by a factor of two to three.

Chicago provides an example of a city which remains centralized in respect to retail employment because much of Chicago's retailing remains thriving within a couple miles of the CBD. Furthermore, peak employment activity at the subcenter location is less than twice that of the CBD. The same is true for sales density except that it peaks seven miles from the CBD. This is significant given that Chicago has a radius of almost forty miles. The centrality of peak density reflects the high rents which continue to prevail throughout central metropolitan Chicago. In addition, the variation in peaks may be explained by the existence of viable older neighborhood shopping areas around central

Chicago that though they afford a high level of employment, do not enjoy the same level of sales activity as do newer retail development in the near western suburbs and around the university districts on the far north and south sides of the city. The t-ratios for the radial gradients increase with the proximity of μ^{**} to the CBD. However, it proves impossible to fit the model at 1 mile due to a lack of variation in μ_1. Furthermore, this and the presence of multicollinearity lead to a failure of the J-test for any distance closer than the 2 and 3 mile pair. Because the first outlying MRC is located at 1.5 miles, it seems reasonable to fix the unascertained peak at 2 miles. Contrastingly, because the location of the estimated sales peak is not near the CBD, the J-test succeeds in ascertaining the location at 7 miles.

Exclusive of Chicago, the average distances of the employment and sales peaks occur midway between the CBD and the furthest MRC. Results for employment density indicate that peak activity occurs at an average of .51 of that radial distance. At this peak, average estimated density is 1.7 times the average employment density at the CBD. Furthermore, results for the sales density studies have indicated that peak activity occurs at an average of .52 of the radial distance. However, at the sales peak, average estimated density is 3.4 times the average sales density at the CBD.

Five SMSAs for employment density and four SMSAs for sales density of the SMSAs studied have peaks beyond the radial mid-point between the CBD and their furthest MRC (column 1). All four of the SMSAs passing the employment density J-test have their employment peaks beyond fifty-percent. The pattern for sales density has more variation. For example, Detroit's peaks occur at 17 and 21 miles for sales and employment, respectively. The results suggest that on average, peak rents occur at distances from downtown Detroit where there exists the most intensive commercial land use. These peaks concur with the locations of Birmingham-Bloomfield Hills, Troy, and Farmington Hills -- three of the highest rent communities in metropolitan Detroit. In general, these peaks occur in the affluent high-rent suburban ring that surrounds the central urban area. Therefore, employment and sales densities appear to serve as appropriate proxies for rent density.

There may exist small sample problems with most of the SMSA studied, because only a few of the cities have a large sample. Of these large sample cities, only Chicago with 50 observations and Detroit with 36 observations pass either of the J-tests (column 14). The other ones passing each have 18 to 29 observations.

For most of the SMSAs, the model fits the data for a wide range of model specifications. However, in a few cases it barely fits or does not fit at all. For example, the model only begins to fit Indianapolis for employment density at the 7-mile specification, while in Philadelphia and Pittsburgh, the model does not fit at all. The employment results for Philadelphia suggest that density declines from the CBD to a minimum and then increase thereafter. The situation does not significantly improve for sales density. Even though the model fits for sales density over a segment of the Philadelphia data, the J-test fails. The problem with the Philadelphia study appears to be two-fold. The data is highly heteroskedastic and two-thirds of the observations are clustered within the first-quartile of radial distance. In part, this may be due to the inclusion of observations from the lower-rent areas on the Camden, New Jersey side of the SMSA. For the case of Pittsburgh, the lack of fit appears to result from geography. Because of the mountainous terrain beyond the first ring of development surrounding the Ohio-Allegheny-Monongahela river valley, there exists a more than seven-mile gap before the appearance of observations in a second ring.

Conversely, the model fits the data for other cities over a wider range of specifications. The model significantly fits the Detroit data at the .025 level from the 8-mile through the 22-mile specifications for both employment and sales densities. It is in such cases that the J-test proves most valuable for identifying peaks.

If there exists a pattern in the outcome of the J-tests, it occurs between the SMSAs which pass the J-test and those which do not. The radial gradients generally appear consistently more significant for these SMSAs than for the ones not passing the test.

Detroit and Washington are the two SMSAs whose results prove most satisfying for both employment and sales density because they produce significant results for both their estimated coefficients at their peak density specification and pass their J-tests at a high level of significance. Furthermore, though the positive radial gradient proves more significant than the negative radial gradient for all four SMSAs passing the J-test for both densities, the pairs of t-ratios for μ_1 and μ_2 appear more balanced with one another for Detroit and Washington than they do for Atlanta and Houston.

Initial employment-density results suggest that Chicago and Indianapolis should pass the J-test. However, both cities have few observations on the short side of their apparent activity peak. As inferred earlier from the Chicago study, cases for which the J-test should otherwise work, fail due to a lack of observations. This shortage of observations results in both the lack of variation for one independent variable and the inoperable problems of multicollinearity. On the other hand, the J-test proves most efficient and useful in cases where peak activity occurs mid-distance and multiple plausible model specifications exist, such as in the Detroit and Washington cases. Therefore, both Chicago and Indianapolis apparently pass the sales density J-test because the peaks occur at a more midway location than they do for employment density.

By their existence, alternative cases such as Philadelphia and Pittsburgh for which the model does not fit for both densities, and cases for which the model fits but does not pass the employment density J-test lend credence to the four SMSAs which pass the test for both densities. Contrastingly, the elasticities for SMSAs failing the test using employment density appear further away from unity than for those passing. However, a similar assessment for sales density does not appear as clear. Further, the elasticities for the SMSAs passing the J-test are generally in the neighborhood of unit elasticity (which is expected in such studies).

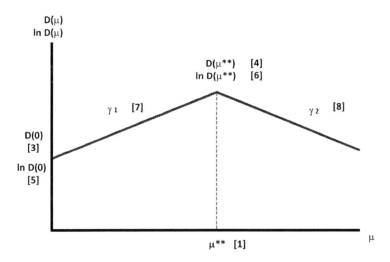

Fig. 13. Employment and Sales Density.
Bracketed Numbers Refer to Columns in Tables 3. and 4.

As evident in the graphs in figure 13, none of these estimates represent an extreme value. The estimated peak densities all fall within the range of actual observations, and are located within the affluent suburban ring surrounding the central city. With the exception of Atlanta, the SMSAs passing both sets of J-tests have their estimated sales peak closer to the CBD than their employment peak which suggests the occurrence of greater average sales-per-employee productivity at the sales peak than at other locations. Because high rents necessitate high productivity on the part of the retailers, these peaks indicate a more intensive land use in these high-rent areas than in surrounding lower-rent locations. For this economic reason and because of the robustness of the sales density model, sales density serves as the better proxy for rent density.

The results for both sets of tests also suggest that peak density laterally occurs at some distance from the highway. In the employment density studies, five of the eight SMSAs for which the model fits have positively-sloped lateral gradients. As with the results for the one-phase model in table 1, these gradients are generally steeper but worse fitting than their respective radial gradients. Consistent with the robustness of the sales density measure, the results indicate positively-sloped lateral gradients for six of the nine cases. As with employment density, these lateral densities are steeper but less significant than their respective radial gradients.

VIII. CONCLUSIONS

It follows from the model and hypothesis developed in sections II and III that one peak of subcenter activity should occur at distance μ^{**} from the CBD. Furthermore, peak subcenter activity may occur at a short lateral distance of ρ^{**} from a radial highway. Therefore in both the employment and sales density functions, evidence of peak subcenter activity should appear as maxima.

The result for the studies utilizing employment density indicates that the two-phase negative-exponential model fits for eight of the ten SMSAs and that their peak of employment activity can be estimated by t-ratios. However, accuracy of these estimates is inversely proportional to the number of plausible competing models. The J-test provides a greater degree of confidence in estimating the true peak, but in the employment density studies, the J-test was only successful in the case of four cities--Detroit, Washington, D.C., Houston, and Atlanta.

In contrast, the results for the sales density studies indicate that sales is the more robust of the two densities. Not only did the model fit in the cases of nine SMSAs, but the J-test was also successful in eight of the cases.

The results for those SMSAs passing the sales J-tests appear more dispersed than for the employment J-tests. However, the average exclusive of Chicago indicates that sales density is located at .52 of the distance between the CBD and the furthest MRC while employment density is located at .51 of the same distance.

There also exists evidence that the lateral location of the peak is some distance from any radial highway. This is evidenced by the signs of the lateral gradient coefficients in column 16. Similar to the reasoning about the radial dimension, a positive coefficient indicates a lateral misspecification which suggests that the true peak of activity is located away from the highway. In the employment density studies, five of the SMSAs have positive values for their lateral gradients while in the sales density studies six of the SMSAs have positive gradients.

CHAPTER 5

I. INTRODUCTION

It appears that there has been an increase in agglomerative subcenter activity over the past four decades in many large metropolitan areas. The history, theory, and empirical results presented in this book suggest that urban sprawl and suburban flight may be recurrent human behavior in urban-regional development. To support this assertion, the theoretical model developed in Chapter 3 has reflected major monocentric models of the past three millennia. Following this development, the empirical work has tested this extended model against observations for ten radially monocentric SMSAs. The functional form of the model alternately has used employment density and sales density as the dependent variable. Using a two-step technique, the results have ascertained the existence and location of peak subcenter activity for employment in four SMSAs and for sales in eight SMSAs. It has followed that sale density is the more robust measure.

This book has developed from a fundamental intuition stemming from cultural tradition as presented in the appendix. Building upon this tradition, this work has used the historical chronicles and analysis found in Chapter 2 to develop the theoretical model in Chapter 3. In turn, the empirical results in Chapter 4 lend support to a theory of peak subcenter activity.

II. HISTORICAL PERSPECTIVE

Throughout the ages, monocentric urban models have provided civilizations with powerful tools for self-analysis and understanding. While writers of each age have relied upon the available communicative tools of their own time and culture, common universal themes underscore all of their works. Though these models vary from age to age, certain elements, such as radiating roads and concentric urban rings, have recurrently appeared. The specific analyses have varied from the prose of Plato, More, and Von Thünen to the mathematics of Lösch, Alonso, and Mills.

The historical treatise leading to the development of the theory in Chapter 3 has demonstrated that facets of many ideal and real monocentric cities dating from primitive times can be used to develop extended models which better address current urban-regional economic issues. Studies of Plato's allegory of Magnesia, Von Thünen's Isolated State, and the contemporary models of Lösch and Mills have proved especially useful towards this development.

III. THEORETICAL PERSPECTIVE

The outgrowth of the historical research has been a revised standard model having a circular plain with a centralized primary business district, a radial partitioning of land, and a surrounding ring with agglomerative subcenters located midway to the urban limit. More specifically, Chapter 3 has developed a bid-rent model in one uniform segment of the general monocentric urban model. The specific model has analyzed competitive bidding between business and residential users. The existence of a small number of radial highways has resulted in business-bid dominance for highway frontage. In addition, competitive bidding between business and residential users has resulted in the development of both a business center and subcenter. The subcenter has developed from the introduction of an avoidance-rent segment into the residential bid-rent function and the emergence of business agglomeration economies.

Especially because of the agglomeration economies, this model has suggested that urban land rents reach a maximum midway from the CBD to the urban limit. This suggestion has formed the premise for the two-phase functional model employed in the empirical study.

IV. EMPIRICAL PERSPECTIVE

It follows from the model developed in the third chapter that one peak of subcenter activity should occur at distance μ^{**} from the CBD and at a short lateral distance of ρ^{**} from a radial highway. Therefore in both the employment and sales density functions, evidence of radial and lateral locations of peak subcenter activity should appear as local radial and lateral maxima.

To ascertain the existence and location of peak retail subcenter activity, this study has employed the two-step technique comprised of a comparative t-test, and a Davidson-MacKinnon J-test, applied to the extended urban model and data for ten SMSAs. Exclusive of Chicago, the average distances of the employment and sales peaks occur midway between the CBD and the furthest MRC. Results for the employment density studies have indicated that peak activity occurs at an average of .51 of that radial distance. At this peak, average estimated density is 1.7 times the average employment density at the CBD. Furthermore, results for the sales density studies have indicated that peak activity occurs at an average of .52 of the radial distance. However, at the sales peak, average estimated density is 3.4 times the average sales density at the CBD.

Sales density works in the J-tests in twice as many cases as does employment density. This suggests that sales density is the more robust measure. In conclusion, the employment and sales densities appear to serve as adequate proxies for rent density. The empirical results affirm the assertions of Plato and others and the mathematical model of Chapter 3.

CHAPTER 6

RESEARCH EXTENDING FROM
THE SPECIFIC MODEL

I. CULTURAL STUDIES

The brief historical study has only touched the surface of a vast amount of interdisciplinary literature existent on this topic. This current work has sketched out a handful of ancient to modern examples which most strongly influence western culture. With more than two millennia of scholarship upon which to draw, this topic could expand to at least one major volume. Furthermore, the history exposes many possible variations of the monocentric model not used in the extended model developed in Chapter 3. One could incorporate these variations into other extended models to address urban situations for which the present extended model or standard model may prove insufficient.

Therefore, one needs to expand the scope of field to other sciences. In the text *Curious Alignments* and addendum videos (previous work by Sase [105]), this author considers numerous ancient monocentric developments. These include those of the Pre-Columbian mound builders in America (also see George R. Milner [106], Henriette Mertz [107], Barry Fell [108, 109], W.B. Hinsdale [110]); the system of Mayan cities in the Yucatan (see Robert J. Sharer [111]; the Alaise Alignments of villages and places in ancient Europe centered in the old Frankish Kingdom (Sase, pp. 47-50 [105]); the early civilizations at Puma Punku (see Vranich [112]; the Incan civilization at Machu Picchu discovered by Bingham in 1911 (see Bingham [113], and the measurement of the earth by ancient civilizations (see Heath and Michell [114]).

II. SUBCENTER MODELS

The third chapter develops an open-city model for the purpose of observing basic subcenter formation and development. However, the model could be reformulated as a closed-city model for the purpose of examining intra-urban dynamics for a fully-mature urban region. In addition, the extended model developed in this book only addresses specific subcenter variations for Retail Trade. Nevertheless, one could also examine specific variations of the effects of suburbanization and agglomeration economies for the Wholesale, Manufacturing, and Service employment sectors.

The empirical work could also be extended. Using new Census of Retail Trade with at the Major Retail Center level and a new edition of the Geological Survey maps or online sources such as Google Earth, this study may be extended to both comparative static and dynamic models. Such a study would lend support to the speculations and intuitive observations made in this paper concerning the locational development of Retail Trade in the affluence of the 1990s, the real-estate bubble and crash of the 2006 onward into the second decade, as well as recovery into the 2020s.

III.   CROSS-MARKET EFFECTS

The fields of Urban/Regional Development and Real Estate Markets have undergone extensive change in the past two decades. Interest rates affect real estate markets. In turn, these market effect urban and regional development. This development does not occur in a vacuum. Rather, there are a series cyclical cross effects in labor markets, residential housing markets, as well as markets for services, retail, wholesale, and manufacturing.

During recent decades, retail, wholesale, and manufacturing markets have moved from localized constraints to globalized constraints. Changes in these markets have had a pronounced effect on the other markets. Therefore, the basic fluctuations for understanding changes across all markets suggests a wider understanding of economic change over short and long periods of time and the cyclic inter-relationships within these changes.

IV. INTEREST RATES AND ECONOMIC CYCLES

Therefore, to understand urban/regional development and real-estate markets, one needs to explore the economic history of financial crises, events that continue to occur and reoccur. Throughout history, both rich and poor countries have muddled their way through a vast range of crises. These crises have included sovereign-government defaults on both domestic and foreign national debts, banking and financial market panics, and collapses due to piracy on the high seas and subprime mortgage meltdowns. In addition, there has been monetary inflation, due to everything from species-currency debasement, which reduced the gold and silver content of coins in favor of more base metals in recent centuries, to the modern corollary of printing more paper money within a network of sovereign fractional-reserve central banks.

Of focused importance to urban/regional development and real-estate markets is the Subprime Mortgage-Backed Securities Bubble burst in 2008. We felt that we had encountered something unheard of in human history. In response to this episode, many in America and around the world denied any connection to past crises and believed instead that this time would be different. However, Reinhart and Rogoff [115] produce evidence that refutes this belief, evidence that is almost a millennium old. The authors cover sixty-six countries across five continents and eight centuries to create their argument that financial disasters are universal behaviors, rites of passage for all countries and nations. Sidney Homer [116] presents an account of interest-rate trends and lending practices that span more than four millennia of economic history. By including evidence from ancient Mesopotamia, Greece, and Rome, the Medieval Times, and Renaissance Europe, he offers a view of the *rise and fall* of empires against the backdrop of the *fall and rise* of their long-run average interest rates. Homer concludes that these rates move inversely to the rise and fall of empires.

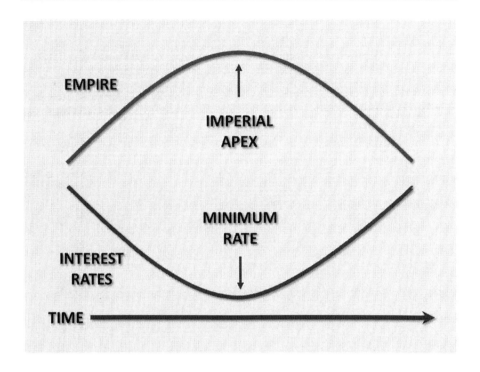

Important to this current discussion, Steiner [117] dates and names the cultural epochs that began with Ancient India in the eighth millennium BCE. These epochs include Persian, Egypto-Chaldean, Greco-Roman, and Anglo-German, among others. All of these epochs are of equal length, approximately 2,200 years.

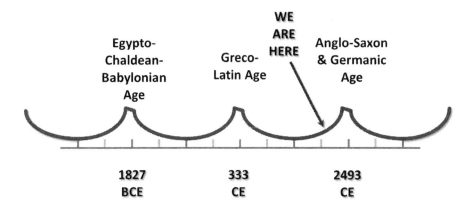

Unfortunately for our present purposes, reliable data on Economics that is currently available dates only to the Sumerian civilization of the Uruk period of the fourth millennium BCE, the middle of the Persian cultural epoch.

Hudson [118] tells us that readable, detailed data in Sumerian economic records only began to appear around 2500 BCE. At this time, which was during the Bronze Age, certain professionals, skilled tradespersons, and managers began to pay a recorded fee to the temples or to the palace. As this system of tithing promulgated throughout the ancient world, the recording of credits of advance payments made and debits of accrued obligations owed needed to be made. As a result, written contracts, pledges of collateral, affidavits of witnesses and sureties were recorded along with publicly regulated rates of interest.

Observations made by Steiner, Homer, Hudson, and others is that mega-cyclic economic changes move in lock-step with the development and decay of empires, across the ages of our human past. Overarching observations of previous economies read as follows: Sweeping economic change reflects the skills and knowledge of a population, its production of goods and services, the behavior of markets and trade, and a myriad of other factors. These float atop an undercurrent of massive and lengthy cyclic changes in agriculture, planetary fluctuations, and our relationship to the sun and companion planets of our solar system against the backdrop of a universe in constant cyclic motion.

Prices and quantities of product, labor and wages, and money and interest rates form markers by which we may gauge fluctuations over lengthy periods of time. Though one may not yet possess the tools to measure the economic fluctuation of cultural epochs accurately, at least one has sufficient methods and data to measure the rise and fall of individual empires.

As mentioned above, Homer [116] offers evidence and explanation in the form of long-run interest rates over the lifespan of these empires. He measures interest rates, ranging from the Sumerian empire through more recent ones. He explains that, though interest rates remain in constant flux, they follow a long-run trend downward as an empire builds to its point of maturity—its golden age. Then, as an empire begins its process of slow decay into the abyss of history, interest rates begin to follow a long-run trend upward.

The simple explanation for this phenomenon in economic terms is *risk*. Risk is associated with uncertainty—uncertainty over time and at a given point of time. The greater the uncertainty, then the greater the perceived level of risk exists. In order to undertake increasing risk, the potential reward must grow correspondingly greater. Hence, the interest rate must be higher than it would be under conditions of greater certainty.

The cycle of empires remains the longest fluctuation that we can measure in meaningful economic terms. The major financial crisis that we observe within the empire cycle is tied to the deterioration of the empire itself. The final phase of collapse often comes in the form of siege and sacking from without after the empire already has been destroyed from within. Nevertheless, most of us are more interested in understanding fluctuations and the occurrence of crises within a smaller window of time. However, given an understanding of cultural-epoch cycles and the shorter empire cycles within each of the former, one can begin to understand the nature of the temporal cycles that is experience within shorter periods of time.

In the discussion of economic cycles and their effect on urban/regional development and real-estate markets, the debate continues as to whether or not shorter cycles are tied to, or, ride upon, longer ones. The Social Science of Economics exists in the space between natural and spiritual sciences. Traditionally, the current permutation of Economics known as Neo-Classical leans heavily upon the concepts borrowed from physics and other natural sciences.

The concept known as the Fourier Harmonic Series is one that we use to measure waves upon the ocean, currents of air, and harmonics in music and color. In Economic Cycle Theory, we apply this concept to the apparent periodicity (recurrence at regular intervals) of different economic cycles. We will treat the physics of harmonics as an analogy or metaphor when applied to series of economic fluctuations.

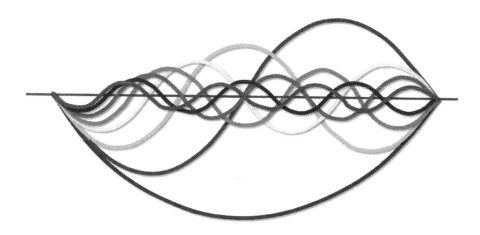

The concept of economic cycles is based upon a theory that attempts to explain changes in business against long-run growth and decay trends as observed in market economies. In determining an economic cycle, we include such variables as growth of Gross Domestic Products, aggregate household income, and labor employment rates, in addition to the factors mentioned earlier. Economists divide the cycles into two main phases, *booms* and *recessions*. Associated with a strong economy, booms are measured as progressions above the long-run trend. In contrast, recessions are characterized by below-trend activity.

In 1939, Schumpeter [119] proposed a typology of business cycles according to their periodicity. Considered by some economists to be components of the harmonic series of economic cycles, the prominent ones include, in descending length: 1) The Nikolai Kondratiev Wave, which reflects a long technological cycle of forty-five to sixty years. His initial measurements determined a fifty-eight-year cycle based upon long-term agricultural prices and wages; currently, the Wave has been adapted to measure changes in technology. 2) The Simon Kuznets infrastructural (building) investment cycle, which reflects changes that have a frequency of fifteen to twenty-five years. 3) The Joseph Kitchin inventory cycle, which is eight to nine years in length, and 4) The Clement Juglar fixed-investment business cycle, which averages 3.3 years.

AVERAGE CYCLE LENGTH

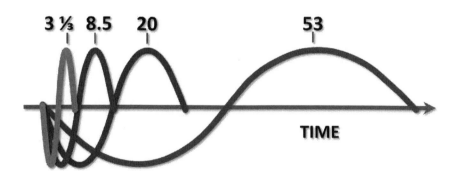

Forrester [120, 121] has spent four decades studying business structure, economic cycles, and national policy. Within the past decade, he and his colleagues have developed and assembled a system-dynamics model of the national economy. Preliminary studies indicate that production sectors generate three different modes of fluctuation in the economic system of the United States. These are similar to the forty-five-to-sixty-year Kondratieff cycle, the fifteen-to-twenty-five-year Kuznets cycle, and the three-to-seven-year business cycle in long-established Cycle Theory.

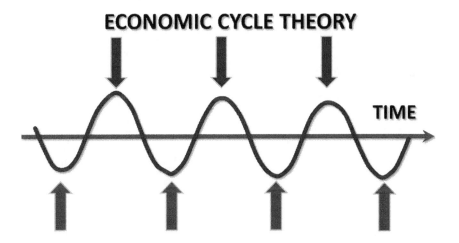

Forrester's empirical results support earlier theories of Economic Cycles. Though Forrester's empirical work focuses on the American economy, his methods can be applied to data from many other countries as well.

In order to understand economic cycles and financial crises and their effect upon urban/regional development and real estate markets, one first must understand the major protagonist and antagonist—the incorporated company. Micklethwait and Wooldridge [122] trace the development of the modern corporation from the thirteenth century to the present. The authors note that the way societies produce, trade, and finance within our epoch increasingly has been a result of the corporate form. Since the development of the Corporation of the City of London a millennium ago, this form of business entity has changed the way that we organize many of our human activities on a global scale. Furthermore, the progression of financial crises throughout recent centuries has attached itself to and conjoined with the development of the modern multi-national corporation. As a result, it is not possible to analyze and to understand the nature and causes of these crises without an understanding of the behavior of this dominant form of business entity.

Furthermore, one also must keep in mind that the major growth spurt in the number and size of corporations has occurred only within the past 250 years. Smith [123] states that a large company in the 18th century employed only twenty-five people. By contrast, Walmart Corporation currently employs more than two million workers globally. Within the financial sector, the number of banks in the United States has decreased while their average size has increased. In 1920, there were almost 30,000 banks in the U.S. Today, less than 8,000 remain. The four largest institutions, Bank of America, J.P. Morgan Case, Citigroup, and Wells Fargo, control half of all bank assets in the United States.

Reich [124] explains corporations. He states, "A final truth that needs to be emphasized--the most basic of all--is that corporations are not people. They are legal fictions, nothing more than bundles of contractual agreements." Reich adds that "[T]he triumph of Supercapitalism has led, indirectly and unwittingly, to the decline of democracy."

Let one explore the five long waves that have occurred over the course of the history of the United States, onward from 1787. Returning to Kondratiev Waves, if we project measurements backward from the 20th century, one finds that the industrial-based and agricultural-based calculations coincide fairly well until the mid-nineteenth century. The first three waves that occurred up to the time of the first great contraction, which is known as the Great Depression of the 1930s can be summarized as follows:

The first wave began during the late 18th century at the time of the American Revolutionary War. It reached its peak during the early decades of the United States. One can identify this wave by the economic prosperity of the time. This is due to maritime trade along with the development and proliferation of Eli Whitney's cotton gin. In addition, the development of the steam engine by James Watt and its application to water transportation by Robert Fulton furthered this prosperity.

The second wave began in the first third of the 19th century during the Era of Good Feeling, a period during the presidency of James Monroe in which Americans were united in purpose. The wave reached its peak about one decade before the War Between the States. One can identify this wave by the prosperity that resulted from the acquisition of California from Mexico and the subsequent California Gold Rush from 1848 to 1859. In addition, the development of the steel industry, which enabled the rapid growth of railroads in the Eastern United States, helps to define this wave.

The third economic wave began around 1880, the time that the United States went to freer silver and gold standards. The wave ends at the time that President Franklin D. Roosevelt took the country off of the gold standard in 1933. One can identify the economic surge of this wave by a series of events. These include the period of Gold Resumption Prosperity; the completion of, and trade along, the First Transcontinental Railroad during the 1880s; the periods of Corporate Merger and Corporate Growth during the decade preceding the First World War; and the urban growth of the Roaring Twenties, which included the stock/bond market bubble that led to the Depression of the 1930s. During this wave, a focus on education and engineering led to massive developments in the fields of electric power and equipment as well as new chemical products. In order to cast a light on the events that occurred during these waves, one can use the science of economic measurement that developed contemporaneously with them.

Within the past two decades, the major financial bubble of the early 1990s occurred in Japan, it should have served as a warning—a specter--for the United States in the late 2000s. The Japanese disaster centered on real estate and stocks. During this bubble, real estate prices increased seventy-five-fold. On paper, this gain represented 20% of the entire wealth in the world. For added perspective, economists often cite that selling the Imperial Palace could have paid for the entire State of California.

Simultaneously, share prices for Japanese firms soared skyward, having increased a hundred-fold over the preceding thirty-five years. Increasing share prices were out of sync with the underlying firm-foundation values of Japanese companies. On average, we expect the Price-to-Earnings ratio to be 15:1. In other words, if a share of stock earns $1.00 per year, the market would value that share at $15.00. However, during the bubble in Japan, Price to Earnings had reached 60:1—four times the normal average.

What caused the bubble in Japan? In respect to stocks, a significant driver was provided by the practice of distorting profits by overstating depreciation while reporting earnings that excluded the poorer performance of subsidiary companies. As a result, adjusted earnings and dividends appeared to be much larger than for foreign counterparts even while actual Japanese profitability declined. In the real-estate market, high rents reflect high population density, restrictive land-use laws, and other conditions. The value of a property and its rent tend to reflect one another at prevailing rates of return. If the expected return on a property is 10% per year and the annual rent is $10,000.00 ($833.00 per month), then the property should be worth about $100,000.00. However, rental income rose far slower than real-estate prices in Japan during the early 1990s. Let us say that rent is only $667.00 per month. If the property is valued at $100,000.00, then the rate of return sinks to 8%.

In addition to problems in the Japanese domestic stock and real-estate markets, a strong Yen made it difficult for Japan to export products because of unfavorable exchange rates. The historically low Japanese interest rates had begun to rise in 1989. This led to a borrowing frenzy and a liquidity boom that precursed the mortgage refinances and equity lines in the United States through the early 2000s. The Japanese central bank responded by restricting credit and raising interest rates. However, these actions contributed to the bursting bubble, a market collapse, and a decade-long recession for Japan.

At the turn of the millennium, the financial markets experienced the largest bubble that ever had occurred up to that time. What distinguished the Internet Bubble from others was its association with both new technologies and new trade opportunities. Essentially, the Internet and its offspring created a cyber-marketplace that significantly changed the way that one does business. Also exceptional is the fact that this bubble set new records. It emerged simultaneously as the greatest creator and the greatest destroyer of wealth: $8 trillion of market value evaporated over a period of months.

During this economic episode, Goldman Sachs proclaimed that investor sentiment was not a long-term risk. Unfortunately, this sentiment proved to be a short-term risk with dire consequences for many investors and companies. The NASDAQ Stock Exchange (originally the National Association of Securities Dealers Automated Quotations) listed the lion's share of Internet and related technology stocks. This is significant because the NASDAQ Index tripled during the boom as Internet-company Price-to-Earnings ratios climbed to over 100:1. However, the new millennium did not show kindness to the market. With the exception of a slight surge after 9/11, stock prices fell steadily-- more than three-fold by early 2002.

For the two preceding decades, the broad-scale high-tech industry recorded gains greater than 18%. By 2000, investor expectation for the future reached 25% or higher. However, the earnings of Cisco and JDS Uniphase grew at 15% per year, even though Cisco surpassed a Price-to-Earnings ratio of greater than 100:1.

Cisco lost 90% of its value when the bubble burst. Other companies, such as Amazon, Lucent Technologies, and Yahoo, lost between 93% and 99% + of their value from the high-water mark of 2000 to the low tide of 2001-02.

Security analysts at Merrill Lynch, Morgan Stanley, and Salomon Smith Barney provided much of the catalyst for the bubble. They based their success on their ability to steer lucrative investment banking business to their firms by promising ongoing, favorable research coverage that would support the Initial Public Offerings (IPOs) in the aftermarket.

Analysts pushed the line that traditional valuation metrics lose relevance during the big-bang stage of an industry, which is a time to be reckless, though rational. Individual stock prices soared while security analysts refrained from biting the hands that fed them—those of their corporate CFOs. Traditionally, analysts rated ten "buys" for every one "sell." However, during this bubble, the ratio of buys-to-sell neared 100:1. "Investment gurus" marching in lockstep helped to convince the public that investing was easy. When the bubble burst, celebrity analysts or others in their firms faced lawsuits, investigations, and SEC fines—even death threats.

By 2001, the United States Secret Service and the SEC had commenced prosecution of more than 5,000 cases in respect to the market structures and conducts that led to the collapse. However, most of their original files were destroyed along with their Manhattan offices in Building 7 of the World Trade Center when it collapsed in the late afternoon of 11 September 2001. As a result, one may never know the extent of the fraud and market manipulation that accompanied fee-based underwriting, cheerleading research and analysis, and the widespread greed that contributed to this very destructive bubble.

In the second decade of this millennium, society struggles through the aftermath of the most recent bubble fueled by Mortgage-Backed Securities, Collateralized Debt Obligations, and other inventions of the best and the brightest quantitative analysts on Wall Street. As one searches to understand the causes, one can take away a few lessons that history has provided. One can trace the causes and effects of financial crises from the days of the Sumerian Empire through the present.

Also, one may learn the lesson that human behavior runs contrary to rational and efficient behavior during economic crises. In other words, more and more credulous investors must be found to keep the financial merry-go-round turning. However, though markets occasionally can be irrational, society should not abandon our age-old sense of firm-foundation values. In every economy throughout history, the market eventually corrects itself, albeit slowly and inexorably. Throughout the ages, anomalies have arisen and markets have become irrational, attracting unwary neophyte investors who suffer heavy losses. Nevertheless, everything comes out in the wash as true values are recognized again by the human participants, eventually.

In conclusion, the reader can draw wisdom about real estate and other markets that effect urban/regional growth and development from Graham [125] who explains that

1. Financial markets are not voting booths but weighing instruments

2. The ways and means of valuation have not changed over time

3. Every piece of real, personal, and intellectual property is worth only the benefit that flows from it

4. Like any other economic crisis, this time is NOT different

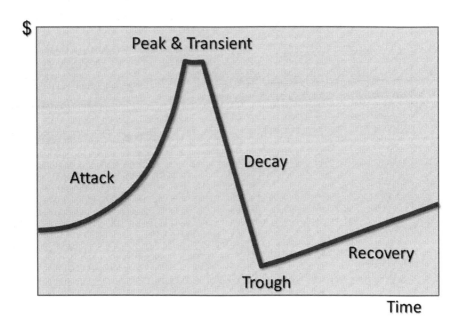

LIFE OF A FINANCIAL CRISIS

V. EARLY DETROIT SUBCENTERS

"Every person who invests in well-selected real estate in a growing section of a prosperous community adopts the surest and safest method of becoming independent, for real estate is the basis of wealth."

--Theodore Roosevelt

This section explores the underpinnings of the Detroit real-estate market and investment therein. From the viewpoint of Urban History, Urban Economics, and Property Law, the field of Real Estate is comprised of elements of all three. To succeed in real estate investment, one must know the history, the scarcity of, and the market demand for the properties. Any form of investment requires a focused study of the market. The real-estate-investment market requires such an application of intelligence and knowledge, especially when the market experiences unstable conditions. If one Googles the word "Detroit" on YouTube, one finds an abundance of videos. Many of these bear such titles as *Detroit in Ruins!*, *Detroit's Ghetto: The Worst Ghetto in the USA*, and *Capital of Scrap: Dying Detroit Looting Itself*. This sensationalism entrances many viewers who dismiss the entire city as one large sewer or garbage heap. However, learned potential investors see opportunity in these properties that have dropped to, or below, their firm-foundation value. Those who know Detroit well realize that most of this YouTube footage focuses on the same isolated parcels on the Lower East Side and Lower West Side of the city. The spread of each of these areas is one to two square miles. In these neighborhoods, the churches and schools have been removed from service and continue to be torn down. More than ninety percent of the homes have been razed or remain uninhabitable due to fire damage.

However, these residences were designed and built to last for only sixty years, the expected length of the automotive boom that began in the 1920s. Therefore, this sequence of events, which economists term Creative Destructionism, is part of a logical progression. Due to the location of these parcels, it makes political and economic sense to prepare them for urban renewal. Contiguous to major rail lines, the residential parcels could be rezoned for commercial use. Nevertheless, most of the investment opportunities exist, or will exist, throughout the remainder of the city. Therefore, potential investors should turn their attention to garnering basic insight as to how more than one dozen submarkets developed geographically and ask what differentiates one from the other?

Throughout history, most cities have developed in much the same way as Detroit. Therefore, as realtor humor goes, the three most important factors about real estate are "location, location, and location."

Many of the enduring cities in the world have rivers running through them: Berlin, Warsaw, Budapest, Paris, London, New York, Chicago, and Detroit are but a few examples. Waterways provide sources of water for drinking and cleaning, routes for low-cost transportation, and barriers for defense. For instance, Paris was rooted on the Isle de Cite in the middle of the River Seine and was accessible only by a number of bridges connecting to the mainland. In the story of Abelard and Heloise, we read that twelfth-century Parisians fought back packs of roaming wolves during the dead of winter along these limited access routes.

What has been called the Cite De Troit (Detroit) in recent centuries began as a settlement that has remained centered at this location since before 800 BCE. In the lesser-known archeological history of Michigan, one finds that the site of the present city as well as its major pathways, the avenues of Jefferson, Michigan, Grand River, Woodward, and Gratiot, date back to at least the civilization of mound-builders that flourished here from a half-millennium BCE to the fourteenth century CE. (Current research produces evidence that many paths converging at Detroit existed during the Copper Culture of 2500 BCE.) When one explores sources like the *Archeological Atlas* of Michigan by Dr. Wilbur B. Hinsdale [126], the hand-drawn survey maps of Douglass Houghton and Bela Hubbard [127] from 1840, and other historical farm atlases of the city, one can detect many Pre-Columbian burial sites in Detroit that have been preserved as part of property occupied by churches and other religious buildings in the modern era. One may surmise that some of the same locational attributes that drew the mound-builders to specific points in the area also attracted the more recent settlers from Europe. Many small towns, villages, and places existed in Wayne County toward the end of the nineteenth century. Of the fifty that were enveloped into the expanding City of Detroit, half were situated along the ancient trails of Grand River, Woodward, and Gratiot Avenues.

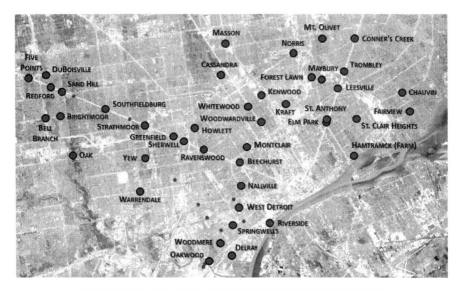

TOWNS AND VILLAGES BEFORE EXPANSION

Some commercial/residential sites in Wayne County flourished, while others vanished. An example of the latter is Maybury, a village near Gratiot Avenue that was founded in the late 1800s. Maybury faded into the property of Detroit City Airport, which opened in 1927.

However, the vestiges of most of the absorbed towns and villages retained their economic importance as neighborhood commercial centers. Even though many of these loci appear dilapidated, their location and other inherent urban-economic attributes continue to provide a significant core for future revitalization. For example, present-day commerce at village sites of Greenfield at the intersection of Grand River and Greenfield, Sand Hill (Old Redford) at Grand River and Lahser, and Griener at Gratiot and Seven Mile remind us that local economic hubs still exist throughout the city.

The precise locales of these economic nodes were established in respect to important travel routes as well as to the quality of surrounding land. A quick study of the *U.S. Geological Survey Maps of 1915* [128] reminds the investigator that Lake St. Clair was once much deeper. It submerged most of Wayne County as well as the southern portions of Oakland and Macomb Counties. Over a course of thousands of years, the periodic retreat of the waters left subsequent belts of sand, clay, and gravel that determined the present quality of the soil. Knowledgeable settler/investors of past centuries determined which sites would sustain large-growth trees, grasslands, or only meager vegetation. These planners also determined the levels of local water-tables along with the resulting probability of recurrent flooding.

Decisions made concerning the location of preferred habitable sites reflected careful study of the inherent conditions and access to least-cost transportation routes. Local zoning combined with winning competitive bids by various classes of commercial and residential developers established the current zoning and recent use of parcels.

VI. RIGHTS-OF-WAY AND INDUSTRIAL PARCELS

Next, let potential planners and investors direct their attention to the major human determinant of local economic development. Before Detroit became known as the Automobile Capital of the World, the city was considered the Railroad Capital of the World. (Before that, lumber was king, following the earlier heyday of fur trapping and processing.)

During the quarter-century that followed the American War Between the States (the Civil War), Detroit factories produced the greatest footage of steel rail of any site in the world. This steel rail was used for the expansion of railroads through the western United States. The rail manufacturers used the Bessemer process, which was brought from Germany to sites along the Detroit River in the late nineteenth century. This process requires a large amount of flowing water for cooling the metal.

Detroit also headquartered the leading producers of steam locomotives, passenger railcars, and other rolling stock. Throughout this era, the present layout of railroad rights-of-way developed as the State of Michigan gave land grants to the existing railway companies in order to encourage economic development of outlying areas of the state. Along the rail-beds, adjacent land was set aside, zoned as industrial property, and sold to the highest commercial bidders who valued the adjacent access to the lines. As a result, ninety percent of the industrial parcels in the city front along the rail lines and ninety percent of the rail corridors are fronted by these industrial tracts.

VII.   URBAN GROWTH

As of 1885, the City of Detroit extended outward a mere three miles from the Central Business District to the first beltway known as East and West Grand Boulevards. Before the city expanded, this pattern was predetermined by the layout of the rail lines and industrial sites. Present-day Detroit grew from the rapid annexation of more than forty established towns, villages, and places. Most of this growth occurred during the First World War through 1926. The placement of rail lines and industrial sites in the late nineteenth century resulted in the partition of the future city into fourteen isolated pockets of varying size.

More than half of these pre-determined urban areas were small ones that developed into blue-collar neighborhoods surrounded by railways and industrial plants. These neighborhoods that contributed to Detroit's early industrialization helped to coin the term "Walk-to-Work Detroit"; workers lived close enough to their places of employment to enjoy a mid-day meal at home before returning to work for another five or six hours.

Two larger areas and two medium-sized ones grew through multiple subdivisions into socio-economically stratified communities. The two medium-sized areas developed before the larger ones. The rectangular area of approximately seven square miles located across from Belle Isle grew first. It is readily identified by its peak neighborhood of Indian Village. As one moves east, west, and north of the Village, the average residence becomes progressively simpler and smaller. Around the periphery of the area adjacent to the industrial parcels, we find small, modest homes that were built as walk-to-work housing. The upper third of this community is demarcated by Gratiot Avenue.

North by northwest of the Central Business District and Cultural Center of the city, a larger community developed. It built upon the burgeoning automotive wealth of the first quarter of the 20th century. This area, encompassing more than fourteen square miles, is identified in respect to three peak neighborhoods. The most prominent of these is known currently as the Boston-Edison Historic and contiguous Arden Park-East Boston Historic Districts. This development straddles Woodward Avenue one mile north of West Grand Boulevard. The mid-sized neighborhood known as Russell Woods is situated southeast of the intersection of Livernois Avenue and Oakman Boulevard. The smallest of these peak neighborhoods is LaSalle Gardens, a community that extends around a residential park to the north of West Grand Boulevard, east of Linwood Avenue.

The two largest tracts of Detroit include the northeast and northwest parts of the city. The major development of these areas occurred during the boom of the 1920s, with delayed expansion after the Second World War. The northeast area encompasses more than thirty-square miles. Technically, the more affluent parts of the northeast are separately incorporated cities: the five Grosse Pointe Communities and Harper Woods. Therefore, the remaining land is part of the City of Detroit. This tract is approximately twenty-square miles. The entire northeast area emerged out of the former Hamtramck Township. This area bore the name of John Francis Hamtramck, second in command to General Anthony Wayne who took possession of the Northwest Territories for the United States after the American Revolution.

Due to the existence of a five-mile-long swamp along Mack Avenue, early surveys and road development reflected pre-British methods of identifying land rights. The formation of long, narrow farms by French habitants resulted in subdivision and street layout that is significantly different than the square-grid pattern prevalent in Northwest Detroit.

In contrast to the Northeast, most of the northwest part of the city and beyond was surveyed under the Public Land Survey System that was developed by Thomas Jefferson. Under this system, square townships of thirty-six square miles were established by measurement in respect to a base line (Eight Mile Road) and a meridian line (Meridian Road, east of Lansing). The survey method divides a standard township into thirty-six sections of one square-mile each. The township is set as a grid of east-west and north-south mile roads. Normally, each mile section is divided into four quarters; half-mile roads are positioned accordingly. The western portion of Northeast Detroit was measured under this newer system in the 1830s as Michigan approached statehood. All of the Northwest Detroit area was measured and subdivided under the Public Land Survey System per the Northwest (Territories) Ordinance of 1787.

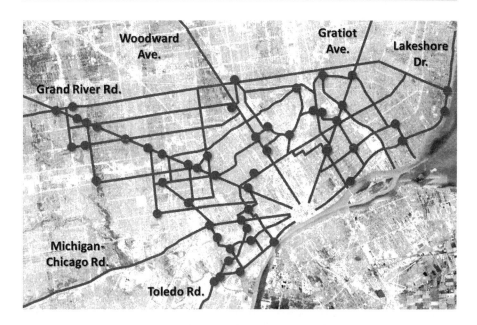

TOWNSHIP AND EARLIER ROAD SYSTEMS

Northwest Detroit remains the largest area of the city. It encompasses approximately fifty square miles of land. Most of the northwest was developed during the automotive boom of the 1920s, with the periphery along the north and west city limits being completed after the Second World War. This wide rectangular part of the city often is viewed as two distinct areas.

Most of the section in the eastern half developed south and westward from a group of peak neighborhoods north of the University of Detroit Mercy and west of the Detroit Golf Club and the former State Fairgrounds. The more affluent neighborhoods include the contiguous subdivisions of Palmer

Woods, Sherwood Forest, and the University District. This half of the northwest area extends westward past Marygrove College to Greenfield Road. The western half of Northwest Detroit emerged out of the northeast portion of Redford Township and is centered at the peak neighborhoods of Rosedale Park and the contiguous South Rosedale and Grandmont communities. Due to geographic proximity, the affluence of this part of Northwest Detroit has been associated with Detroit Diesel and the former American Motors Corporation and Massey-Ferguson Tractor plants.

VIII. THE CITY CHARTER

In order to avoid omission, researchers should take the cities of Highland Park and Hamtramck into account. Both cities were able to remain independent during the period of rapid expansion by Detroit that engulfed other towns and villages. These cities retained their status because the City of Detroit Charter requires that Detroit must completely surround an entity in order to incorporate it involuntarily into the City of Detroit. However, Highland Park and Hamtramck are joined together along a small piece of property that used to be known as Kenwood, a station-stop along the former Grand Trunk Railroad. As neither Hamtramck nor Highland Park can be surrounded individually, neither can be incorporated into Detroit, involuntarily. This situation has remained a point of legal contention for almost a century.

Therefore, what finally determined the geographic growth and development of the city? From our discussion, we may conclude that it was due to the riverside (strait-side) location and inherent soil conditions, the Pre-Columbian radial-road system, the mixture of survey methods and resulting surface-street layout, and the rail and industrial development of the late nineteenth century.

As a whole, the city is viewed by some observers as a cluster of contiguous sub-cities, each with its own social, political, and economic diversity. Therefore, rather than considering the Detroit real-estate market as a homogeneous unit, it may be wise to approach it geographically as a number of separate sub-markets.

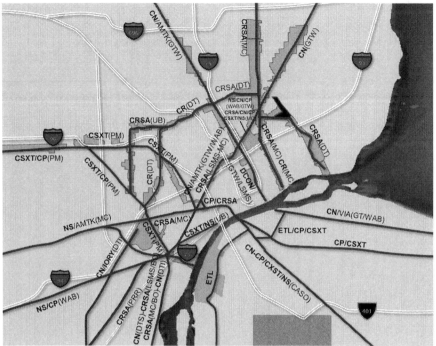

RAILWAYS AND INTERSTATE HIGHWAYS

IX. TAX BASE AND PROPERTY VALUES

Presently, the City of Detroit and the County of Wayne hold an excessive number of unproductive properties in their tax portfolios. Furthermore, taxes for productive (non-abandoned residential and commercial) properties have grown disproportionately for taxpayers in respect to market values. Hence, the common goal for property owners and local government is to increase the market value of city properties and to restore nonproductive ones to the tax role. There is no single, simple solution to this problem as property values and the city/county tax base depend upon commercial and residential demand for land and buildings. Commercial demand reflects sustainment of present businesses and the development of new ones. Conjointly, residential demand rises and falls with employment opportunities.

Fossilization (in which major advancements in product and process slow down) has caused the automotive industry to spread throughout the world. The automotive and related industries have advanced technologically, thus requiring a higher-skilled labor force. Though significantly smaller, the automotive industry in Detroit will continue to play a major, though limited, role in the local economy. Alternatively, area companies in biotechnology, computers, and other fields continue to grow and to fill a portion of the basic-industry gap.

Alternatively, numerous institutions of higher education increasingly provide opportunities for international students in an affordable "college-town" atmosphere. Furthermore, the larger institutions continue to grow as centers of research and development. Also, many large hospital systems have taken an advancing role in medical research and education in addition to patient care. Finally, other opportunities in the fields of freight transportation and logistics have appeared and are poised for growth. This effort promises to help Southeast Michigan to develop into the inland port of the freight system that extends through Canada to the deep-water, cargo-container port at Halifax Nova Scotia.

What real estate investors, planners, and developers need to understand is that Detroit probably will not experience a rapid turnaround. Such a turnaround would be atypical for most cities. The opportunities mentioned in the preceding paragraph will develop slowly. In respect to both commercial and residential demand, Detroit cannot expect to return to a substantial income-base that was supported previously by hundreds of thousands of high-paying, semi-skilled manufacturing jobs. Detroit can and probably will redevelop, eventually. However, this turnaround can only happen through the development a workforce that possesses high levels of education, knowledge, and world-class competitive skills. Apart from a limited number of low-paying, lower-skilled local-economy jobs, there exists little likelihood of sustainable employment for anyone without the acumen that employers locating in Southeast Michigan need to survive in the highly competitive global markets throughout the 21st century.

X. GLOBAL ADVANTAGE

In taking this research agenda toward urban redevelopment, this section considers the economics of location in respect to trade. As with most major cities, Detroit, Montreal, and Halifax share locational advantages in respect to global trade. Detroit and Southeastern Michigan along the section Great Lakes Seaway from Port Huron at the southern end of Lake Huron and Grosse Isle Island at the northwestern end of Lake Erie form an expansive international border with Canada. Montreal, Quebec sits at the midpoint between Detroit and Atlantic Ocean and serves as both an international seaport along the St. Lawrence River as well as being the junction of all Canadian railways running east and west. Halifax, Nova Scotia sits buffered by a number of islands along the Atlantic Coast. Because of ocean currents and related environmental factors, Halifax serves as the home of the Canadian Navy and as the year-round deep-ocean port for eastern Canada.

The Great Lakes Global Freight Gateway (GLGFG) project [129], a U.S./Canadian initiative, seeks to develop an inland port and global-freight trade route from Southeast Michigan/Southwest Ontario through Halifax, Nova Scotia, by rail. From there, the route would go to the rest of the world. The establishment of this line would reduce shipping time to and from the American Midwest from two to eleven days, depending on its starting point, thus lowering costs. In addition, this route reduces costs because of the economies of scale that are created by the

largest of the ocean-going container ships that can access the Port
of Halifax.

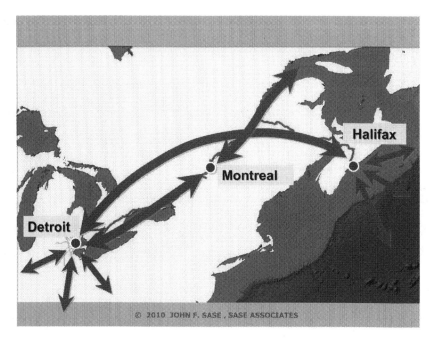

DETROIT-HALIFAX TRADE ROUTE

The GLGFG project has emerged as a major initiative to
restore economic vitality to the Great Lakes region, to the State
of Michigan, and to Metropolitan Detroit. The Great Lakes
Global Freight Gateway not-for-profit corporation takes its
membership from public and private organizations and academia
in the United States and Canada. The GLGFG organization has
projected that the establishment of this route will bring more than
one-hundred sustainable jobs to the Detroit area.

Over the past half a decade, the group has grown in number from a handful to more than four dozen. The principal founder of the GLGFG project, Dr. Michael H. Belzer is also a Transportation Economist at Wayne State University.

From the Pre-Columbian Age through the heyday of the automobile, history regards Detroit and its environs as the ideal North-American location for freight transshipment. (Transshipment is the shipment of goods or containers to an intermediate destination and then to another destination.) Many traders and manufacturers bestow this laurel upon the region of Southeast Michigan because it offers a central location of narrow international crossings to carriers on water, land and in the air that allows them to reach the global marketplace. Modern developments enhance the quality of this inland site, which sits along a global-trade route. The region provides available land along many railroad right-of-ways as well as access to the Interstate and Interprovincial highway systems. These systems provide truck carriers with availability from all directions. Residents of Southeast Michigan/Southwest Ontario have the regional location factor; what they need are jobs for their labor force. Therefore, the economic redevelopment in this region needs to move forward.

Roger Lane, a founding member of the GLGFG team and a former executive of DTE, states, "We are seeing a rare opportunity here in Southeast Michigan. If we do not take advantage of this situation now, we may not have another chance to put the region back in the center of the global economy for many years." He further says that if Michigan does not act to initiate the GLGFG project, secondary sites within the Midwest will.

GLOBAL TRADE ROUTES TO THE GREAT LAKES

From a Google-Earth view of 1,500 miles, one can recognize that the a project of this economic scale can serve as a means to develop an expansive, coordinated, multimodal (rail, truck, sea, and air) trade route between the heart of North America and Europe, Africa, the Middle East, and Southeast Asia. Such a development will move the region toward the center of the global-trade network and will spur revitalization of the economy on and around the Great Lakes. These events will transpire because the GLGFG links the deep-water port of Halifax, Nova Scotia, to the transshipment-distribution hub in Southeast Michigan by existent Canadian rail. The rail-line runs along the banks of the St. Lawrence Seaway.

A group of fifty professionals from business, government, and academia on both sides of the border has taken the GLGFG from concept to its current status as the focal point of the Great Lakes Gateway, a Michigan not-for-profit corporation (GLG). With a consortium of planning and management teams, the GLG reflects expertise in business, economics, finance, law, industrial relations, regional planning, real estate and commercial development, communications, labor, and government.

As its core function, the GLG serves as an economic management forum that espouses the stated mission of bringing together freight transporters and cargo owners through the coordination and utilization of existing and future freight facilities and components. Through its actions, the Michigan-based GLG continues to develop cooperation with Canadian entities that include the government-sponsored, not-for-profit Halifax Port

Authority, which oversees the deep-water port and cargo-loading and -unloading facilities at Halifax and the privately owned CN Railway (formerly known as the Canadian National Railway), with its rail lines, depots, and existing facilities in Southeast Michigan. In addition, this GLGFG plan outlines the benefits offered by the current freight corridor, which extends from Michigan to the Halifax port in order to reach the markets in Europe, the Middle East, and beyond. Furthermore, the GLG sees the development of an additional rail-freight corridor between Detroit and Montreal as well as a freight corridor to the Far East from British Columbia ports.

The Great Lakes Global Freight Gateway remains a work in progress that focuses on the enhancement of the Southeast Michigan international-inland port. Given the existing facilities, the plan emphasizes that the GLG can launch operations in order to double the flow of cargo rapidly between Michigan and Nova Scotia. Belzer states, "The beauty of this plan is that so much of the infrastructure is already in place. The project doesn't need a study. It doesn't need massive planning. It doesn't need much in the way of legislative or governmental approval. The elements of the project only need to be coordinated, linked, and then managed smoothly. It's ready to implement and execute."

At full operational capacity, the GLG has projected that this public/private economic initiative could generate $11 billion of new economic activity while adding 150,000 sustainable jobs. These jobs would center in the employment sectors of freight transportation, warehousing, and logistics. In addition, the initiative may produce positive-spillover effects to many other industries as the GLGFG project complements and helps to revitalize, not replace, existing manufacturing industries throughout the Great Lakes region. The GLG informs us that the GLGFG is a strategic plan that reduces international-shipping time while lowering freight-transshipment costs. It provides a sustainable and earth-friendly system for producers, shippers, and the public at large. GLG teams have met with potential shippers and other stakeholders to develop their joint strategies as well as individual-value propositions. The objective is to provide assurance of swifter global-freight transport as well as lower total shipping costs in the movement of their goods. Note: Demand for global transshipment represents a derived demand of freight to be carried. If the freight itself contains intermediate goods, then in turn the demand for these goods are a derived demand of the demand for the final product

In the medium-run, container-freight volume may increase by measurable amounts throughout the region. GLG predicts that container traffic on the CN Railway can double from 45,000 to 90,000 container lifts (lifting a cargo container unit from one mode of transportation and placing it on another). As a result, shipping costs per container would decrease due to the increased economies of scale and greater regulatory coordination between the two sovereign governments. This projection assumes that cargo owners and their agents enter into agreements, ones that will shift more freight to the Halifax-Great Lakes.

Assuming that cargo volume can reach 100,000 containers, the goal for Detroit operations, the CN Railway will have neared its maximum local capacity. As a result, the increasing flow of containers would bolster demand to expand the present facilities and to develop a few more transshipment sites in and around the Detroit Metropolitan Region. Forecasts made in conjunction with the Center for Automotive Research (C.A.R.) [130] indicate that investment demand for funds to finance the construction of a number of new logistics parks (high-tech routing warehouses and yards) and investment in intermodal-distribution centers could reach $2 billion, depending on the size and functionality of the sites.

The GLG has set a target volume of 400,000 containers, measured as twenty-foot equivalent units (TEUs). As freight volumes increase to 200,000 containers on board the CN, along with another 200,000 by way of the other existent railroads, the heightened capacity requirements will lead to additional, extensive investment. Dr. Belzer asserts that "just reaching 100,000 units will create substantial economic activity and employment. As we increase mass, we decrease cost and improve service, thus creating a Virtuous Cycle of Economic Development (a complex system of economic events that reinforces itself through a feedback loop)."

Assuming that near-run objectives are met, early estimates indicate that shipping from Halifax to the Great Lakes would be faster, greener, and less expensive than movement by alternative routes. Depending on alternate port of entry and final destination, the Halifax-Great Lakes route will cut between $250 and $930 of total-landed cost per container. Note: The new generation ocean-container ships include twenty Triple-Es that have been ordered by the Maersk shipping line. Each of these vessels can carry from 15,000 to 18,000 ocean-going containers. Given the upper-end capacity, the aforementioned estimates translate to savings of $4.5 to $16.7 million per shipload.

In addition, loading containers for export with raw and processed agrarian goods will increase the cost advantage of using the Southeast Michigan port. In Western Michigan, the advantage will stimulate the formation of partnerships, which will be attractive to agribusinesses as well as to manufacturers. The GLG determines that companies moving 1,000 containers in the course of a year may save as much as $1 million by using the Halifax-Great Lakes route.

The establishment of the Great Lakes Global Freight Gateway matches the launch of a new generation of ocean-going container ships. The Halifax-Great Lakes path provides competitive advantage stemming from the fact that most of the ports in North America lack the depth to accommodate the Super Post-Panamax ships. Apart from the Port of Norfolk, Virginia, the year-around, ice-free port in Halifax remains the only one along the East Coast that can handle this new class of ship. In Halifax, the CN maintains its eastern terminus on the container-terminal piers.

Along with the further development of freight-handling employment, the GLGFG project facilitates the expansion of container-freight volume. Meanwhile, the GLG works with transshipment systems, government agencies in the U.S. and Canada, and freight shippers around the world. However, the GLG does not have plans of its own for local transportation initiatives. Instead, it defines its role as bringing together existing projects developed by other public and private organizations, which network as colleagues in the GLG work to create a unified one-stop-shop for the transport of freight through, to, and from the Great Lakes region.

The GLG vision builds upon TranslinkeD, an earlier concept put forth by the Detroit Regional Chamber. In order to increase rail-freight volumes, the GLG includes present assets as well as new projects, such as further expansions at the Wayne County Aerotropolis (the area in which the layout, infrastructure, and economy are centered around Detroit Metro and Willow Run airports) and bridges and tunnels crossing the strait. In underscoring this statement, the GLG will not take on the role of builder of bridges, tunnels, or other new infrastructure that are vital to the project. Lane states, "That's for others to deal with. We do not care who builds what, or whether it is a bridge or a tunnel. Our mission is to facilitate the movement of many more containers in and out of Southeast Michigan through partnership with our Canadian colleagues in Windsor and Halifax. What happens at the Detroit River is crucially important to us but, frankly, we will be generating enough additional cargo to help defray the cost of whatever is decided. We just want to see it done in a timely manner."

The GLG plan remains a nonpartisan initiative that has been submitted to the Office of Governor of Michigan. Members of GLG engage in ongoing dialogue with this office. In order to implement the project fully, the public and private organizations involved will need to take the analysis, forecasting, and strategic planning beyond the preliminary stages.

APPENDIX

Davidson and MacKinnon [18] suggest a linearized version of the Cox-test statistic. Given the regression

$$(44) \quad H_0: y_i = f_i(X_i, \beta_0) + \varepsilon_{0i}$$

where y_i is the ith observation on the dependent variable, X_i is a vector of observations on exogenous variables, β_0 is a k vector of parameters to be estimated, and the disturbance term ε_{0i} is normally and independently distributed, one can formulate the alternative regression as

$$(45) \quad H_0: y_i = g_i(Z_i, \beta_1) + \varepsilon_{1i}$$

where Z_i is a vector of observations on exogenous variables, and β_1 is an l-vector of parameters to be estimated, and ε_{1i} is normally and independently distributed if H_1 is true. One must assume that H_1 is not nested within H_0 and that H_0 is not nested within H_1. Therefore, the truth of H_0 implies the falsity of H_1, and vice versa.

Davidson and MacKinnon consider embedding the alternative hypotheses in a general model that uses a mixing parameter λ in the combined statistical model

$$(46) \quad y_i = (1 - \lambda)\, f_i\,(X_i,\, \beta_0) + \lambda \hat{g}_i + \varepsilon_i$$

Where $g\ bar\ _i = g_i(Z_i,\ \beta\ bar\ _1)$ and $\beta\ bar\ _1$ is the Maximum-Likelihood estimate of β_1 such that

$$(47) \quad y_i = (1 - \lambda)\, X_i\, \beta_0 + \lambda Z_i \beta_1 + \varepsilon_i$$

Under hypothesis H_1, Davidson and MacKinnon replace the unknown $Z_i\, \beta_1$ with its estimate $Z_{i1} = (I - M_1)y$. Therefore, one may rewrite equation 45 as

$$(48) \quad y_i = (1 - \lambda)\, X_i\, \beta_0 + \lambda Z_i \hat{\beta}_1 + \varepsilon_i$$
$$= (1 - \lambda)\, X_i\, \beta_0 + \lambda \hat{y}_1 + \varepsilon_i$$

If hypothesis H_0 is true in this form, then the true value of λ is zero.

Since $\bar{y}_i$ is asymptotically independent of ε, Davidson and MacKinnon suggest testing whether $\lambda = 0$ in equation 48 by using a conventional t-test which they name the J-test (Judge [47]). In this test, the t statistic from equation 48 is conditional on the truth of H_0, not the truth of H_1. Therefore, the t statistic which is valid for testing the truth of H_0 will not be valid for testing the truth of H_1. If one desires to test H_1, they suggest that one should simply reverse the roles of H_0 and H_1 and repeat the test (Davidson and MacKinnon [18]).

GLOSSARY OF MATHEMATICAL SYMBOLS

β lateral disamenity residential-rent gradient

γ radial business-rent gradient

ζ lateral business-rent gradient

ρ lateral distance along circular streets

$\bar{\rho}$ ρ bar, lateral distance of the urban limit

ρ' lateral distance of closest local maximum of the agricultural and residential rent curves

ρ^* rent equilibrium point between business and agriculture or between business and residential users

ρ_M lateral distance of the mid-line between radial highways

$\dot{\rho}_M$ lateral mid-line distance at the radial boundary of the inner urban district

ρ^+ lateral center of agglomeration

τ lateral normal residential-rent gradient

ψ radial residential-rent gradient

AC   post-agglomeration average cost

C   pre-agglomeration constant average cost

c   (exponent) radial production-density gradient

D   disamenities

n   (exponent) of the avoidance-rent phase function

P_G premium of agglomeration

Q   quantity of production of a large firm

q   quantity of production of a small firm (section IV.)

R   rent

$\bar{R}$ R bar, constant non-urban rent

R_B business rent (an envelope function of normal and premium business rents)

R_{BG} business rent received under agglomeration conditions

R_{BN} normal business rent

R_{BP} premium business rent

R_R residential rent (an envelope of the disamenity refund and normal rent)

R_{RD} residential disamenity refund

R_{RN} lateral normal-residential rent

t   (exponent) lateral production-density gradient

μ radial distance along highway

$\bar{\mu}$ μ bar, radial distance of the urban limit

$\mu^{\bullet}$ radial boundary of the inner urban district

μ^{+} center of agglomeration in subcenter

μ^{*} radial distance at which the avoidance-rent phase begins

μ^{**} radial distance at which the avoidance-rent phase ends

μ' radial distance at which the residential area emerges

μ'' radial distance at which the business center ends

μ''' radial distance at which the business subcenter begins

μ'''' radial distance at which business subcenter ends

REFERENCES

1] James Adam. *The Republic of Plato*, pages 214-215. Cambridge: University Press, 1902 and 1969.
William Alonso. *Location and Land Use*. Cambridge: Harvard University Press, 1964.
[2] Pages 30-33.
[3] Pages 49-52.
[4] Pages 145-157.

5] St. Augustine. *The City of God*, translated and edited by Marcus Dods, D.D., pages vii-xii. New York: Hafner Publishing Co., 1948.

6] M.J. Beckmann and J.F. Thisse. "The Location of Production Activities," Ch 2. of the *Handbook of Regional and Urban Economics, Volume I: Regional Economics*, Peter Nijkamp, editor, pages 80-83. New York: American Elselvier Publishing Co., 1986.

7] Bruce Bender and Hae-Shin Hwang. "Hedonic Housing Price Indices and Secondary Employment Centers," page 90. *Journal of Urban Economics* XVII (1):90, 1985.

8] Ralph M. Braid. *Central and Non-Central Agglomeration of Firms on Single and Intersecting Roadways*, manuscript. New York: Department of Economics, Columbia University, 1987.

9] Ralph M. Braid. "Heterogeneous Preferences and Non-Central Agglomeration of Firms," *Regional Science and Urban Economics* XVIII (1):57-68, 1988.

Robert S. Brumbaugh. *Plato's Mathematical Imagination*. New York: American Book-Stratford Press, Inc., 1954.
[10] Page 6.

[11] Pages 57-58.

12] Tommaso Campanella. *The City of the Sun,* 1623, translated by Daniel J. Donno, pages 27-33. Berkeley: University of California Press, 1981.

13] Joseph Campbell. *The Inner Reaches of Outer Space,* page 38. New York: Harper and Row, 1986.

14] Francis MacDonald Cornford. *Plato's Cosmology: The Timaeus of Plato,* pages vii-xii. New York: Humanities Press, 1937.

15] Francis MacDonald Cornford. *The Republic of Plato,* pages v-ix. The Clarendon Press, 1945.

16] D.R. Cox. "Tests on Separate Families of Hypotheses," *Proceedings of the Fourth Berkeley Symposium on Mathematical Statistics and Probability* I: 105-123. Berkeley: University of California Press, 1961.

17] D.R. Cox. "Further Results on Tests of Separate Families of Hypotheses," *Journal of the Royal Statistical Society,* B24:406-424, 1962.

18] Russell Davidson and James G. MacKinnon. "Several Tests for Model Specification in the Presence of Alternative Hypotheses," *Econometrica* XLIX (3):781-793, 1981.

19] Robin A. Dubin and Chein-Hsing Sung. "Spatial Variation in the Price of Housing: Rent Gradients in Non-Monocentric Cities," *Urban Studies* XXIV: 193-204, 1987.

20] Micea Eliade. *The Sacred and the Profane,* pages 34-58. New York: Harper and Row, 1959.

21] Rodney A. Erickson and Michael Wasylenko. "Firm Relocation and Site Selection in Suburban Municipalities," *Journal of Urban Economics* VIII(1):69-85, 1980.

22] Gordon R. Fisher and Michael McAleer. "Alternative Procedures and Associated Tests of Significance for Non-Nested Hypotheses," *Journal of Econometrics* XVI: 109, 1981.

23] James R. Follain and Stephen Malpezzi. "The Flight to the Suburbs: Insights Gained from an Analysis of Central City vs. Suburban Housing Costs," *Journal of Urban Economics* IX (3): 381-398, 1981.

24] D.H. Fowler. *The Mathematics of Plato's Academy*, pages 364-371. Oxford: Clarendon Press, 1987.

Jurgen Friedrichs and Allen C. Goodman. *The Changing Downtown: A Comparative Study of Baltimore and Hamburg.* Berlin and New York: W. de Gruyter, 1987.
[25] Page 79.
[26] Pages 201-224.

27] Masahisa Fujita. "A Monopolistic Competition Model of Spatial Agglomeration: A Differentiated Product Approach," *Regional Science and Urban Economics* XVIII(1):87-126, 1988.

28] Masahisa Fujita and Francisco L. Rivera-Batiz. "Agglomeration and Hetegeneity in Space: Introduction," *Regional Science and Urban Economics* XVIII(1):1-6, 1988.

David Furley. *The Greek Cosmologists,* Volume I. Cambridge: Cambridge University Press, 1987.
[29] Pages 24-28.
[30] Pages 54-57.

31] Charles N. Glaab and A. Theodore Brown. *A History of Urban America*, page 154. New York: Macmillan Publishing Co., 1976.

32] Allen C. Goodman. *Neighborhood Effects, Hedonic Prices and the Residential Housing Choice*, dissertation. New Haven: Yale University, 1976.

33] Allen C. Goodman. "Externalities and Non-Monotonic Price-Distance Functions," *Urban Studies* XVI:321-328, 1979.

34] Allen C. Goodman and Robin A. Dubin. "Sample Stratification With Non-Nested Alternatives: Theory and A Hedonic Example," *The Review of Economics and Statistics* LXXII: 169-170, 1990.

35] Allen C. Goodman and Robin A. Dubin. "unpublished manuscript." Detroit: Wayne State University, Department of Economics, 1991.

36] David M. Grether and Peter Mieszkowski. "The Effects of Nonresidential Land Uses of the Prices of Adjacent Housing: Some Estimates of Proximity Effects," *Journal of Urban Economics* VIII91):1-15, 1980.

37] A. Grimaud. "Agglomeration Economies and Building Height," Journal of Urban Economics XXV (1): 17-31, 1989.

38] Peter Hall. *World Cities*, pages 59-94. New York: McGraw-Hill, 1966.

39] P.G. Hoel. "On the Choice of Forecasting Formulas," *Journal of the American Statistical Association* XLII: 605-611, 1947.

40] H. Hotelling. "The Selection of Variates for Use in Prediction with Some Comments on the General Problem of Nuisance Parameters," *Annual of Mathematical Statistics*. XI: 271-283, 1940.

41] Ebenezer Howard. *Garden Cities of Tomorrow,* 1898, plan 7. London: Faber & Faber, 1945.

John of Patmos. "The Book of Revelations," *The Holy Bible.*
[42] 1:12-20.
[43] 4:1-4.
[44] 4:11.
[45] 7:3-8.
[46] 9:16.

47] George G. Judge et al. *The Theory and Practice of Econometrics,* page 884. New York: John Wiley and Sons, 1985.

48] Tjalling Koopmans and Martin Beckmann. "Assignment Problems and the Location of Economic Activities," *Econometrica* XXV: 53-76, 1957.

49] Claude Nicholas Ledoux. *L'Architecture Consideree Sous le Rapport de l'Art, des Moeurs et de la Legislation,* pages 72-77. Paris: Chez l'Auterer, 1804, Microfilm. New York: Columbia University Libraries, 1974.

August Lösch. *The Economics of Location.* New Haven: Yale University Press, 1954.
[50] Pages 36-37.
[51] Pages Page 106, figure 1.
[52] Pages 124-126.

53] Kevin Lynch. *Good City Form,* pages 373-389. Cambridge: MIT Press, 1970.

54] Molly MaCauley. "Estimation of Recent Behavior of Urban Population and Employment Density Gradients," *Journal of Urban Economics* XVIII (2):251-260, 1985.

55] Neil S. Mayer. "The Impacts of Lending, Race, and Ownership on Rental Housing Rehabilitation," *Journal of Urban Economics* XVII(3): 349-374, 1985.

56] Michael McAleer. "Specification Tests for Separate Models: A Survey," In M.L. King and D.E.A. Giles (eds.) *Specification Analysis in the Linear Model,* page 147. London: Routledge and Kegan Paul, 1987.

Ernest G. McClain. *The Pythagorean Plato.* York Beach: Nicolas-Hays, 1984.
[57] Page 10.
[58] Page 14.
[59] Pages 47-55.

60] John F. McDonald. *Economic Analysis of an Urban Housing Market,* pages 169-182. New York: Academic Press, 1979.

61] John F. McDonald. "The Identification of Urban Employment Subcenters," *Journal of Urban Economics* XXI(2):245, 1987.

62] John F. McDonald and H. Woods Bowman. "Some tests of Alternative Urban Population Density Functions," *Journal of Urban Economics* III (3): 242-252, 1976.

63] John F. McDonald and H. Woods Bowman. "Land Value Functions: A Reevaluation," *Journal of Urban Economics* VI (1):25-41, 1979.

Edwin S. Mills. *Studies in the Structure of the Urban Economy.* Baltimore: John Hopkins Press, 1972.
[64] Pages 5-9.
[65] Pages 36-55.
[66] Page 82.
[67] Page 88.
[68] Page 98.

69] Edwin S. Mills and Bruce W. Hamilton. *Urban Economics*, page 21. Glenview, Boston, and London: Scott, Foresman and Co., 1989.

Thomas More. *Utopia*, 1516, edited by Edward Surtz S.J. New Haven and London: Yale University Press, 1964.
[70] Page 53.
[71] Pages 59-68.

72] Leon Moses and Harold F. Williamson Jr. "The Location of Economic Activity in Cities," *American Economic Review* LVII: 211-222, 1967.

73] Ryohei Nakamura. "Agglomeration Economies in Urban Manufacturing Industries: A Case of Japanese Cities," *Journal of Urban Economics* XVII (1): 108-124, 1985.

74] Otto Neugebauer. *The Exact Sciences in Antiquity*, page 35. Princeton: Princeton University Press, 1952.

75] Robert E. Park and Ernest W. Burgess. *The City*, page 51. Chicago: The University of Chicago Press, 1925, 1967.

76] Anthony H. Pascal and John J. McCall. "Agglomeration Economies, Search Costs, and Industrial Location," *Journal of Urban Economics* VIII (3):383-388, 1980.

77] M.H. Pesaren. "On the General Problem of Model Selection," *Review of Economic Studies* XL: 155, 1974.

Plato. *The Republic*, translated by F.M. Cornford. New York: Oxford University Press, 1957.
[78] Verse 424a.
[79] Verse 617.

Plato. *Timaeus and Critias,* translated by H.D.P. Lee. Baltimore: Penguin Books, 1971.
[80] Critias, verses 109-113.
[81] Timaeus, verse 47a.

82] Plato. *The Laws,* translated by A.E. Taylor, verses 702-878. New York: E.P. Dutton and Co., Inc., 1960.

83] R.E. Quandt. "The Estimation of the Parameter of a Linear Regression System Obeying Two Separate Regimes," *Journal of the American Statistical Association* LIII: 873-880, 1958.

84] Rand McNally Co. Metropolitan, city, and county-street and road maps, assorted.

85] Harry W. Richardson. "On the Possibility of Positive Rent Gradients," *Journal of Urban Economics* IV (1): 60-68, 1977.

86] Harry W. Richardson. *Urban Economics,* page 53. Hinsdale, Illinois: The Dryden Press, 1978.

87] Francisco L. Rivera-Batiz. "Increasing Returns, Monopolistic Competition, and Agglomeration Economies in Consumption and Production," *Regional Science and Urban Economics* XVIII (1): 125-154, 1988.

88] A.D. Roy. "A Further Statistical Note on the Distribution of Individual Output," *Economic Journal* LX: 831-836, 1950.

89] Paul A. Samuelson. "Thunen at Two Hundred," Journal of Economic Literature XXI:1470-1475, 1983.

90] E. Segelhorst and M. Brady. "A Theoretical Analysis of the Effect of Fear on the Location Decisions of Urban-Suburban Residents," *Journal of Urban Economics* XV (2): 157-171, 1984.

91] Robert Sinclair. *The Face of Detroit, A Spatial Analysis,* page 39. Detroit: Department of Geography, Wayne State University, 1972.

92] Daniel B. Suits, Andrew Mason, and Louis Chan. "Spline Functions Fitted by Standard Regression Methods," *The Review of Economics and Statistics* LV:132-139, 1978.

93] Helen Tauchen and Ann D. Witte. "Socially Optimal and Equilibrium Distributions of Office Activity: Models with Exogenous and Endogenous Contacts," *Journal of Urban Economics* XV(1):66-86, 1984.

94] A.E. Taylor. *A Commentary on Plato's Timaeus,* Oxford: The Clarendon Press, 1928.

95] U.S. Government, Bureau of the Census. 1982 Census of Retail Trade, Major Retail Centers in SMSAs.

96] U.S. Government, Department of Interior. U.S. Geological Survey Maps, 1980.

Johann Heinrich Von Thunen. *The Isolated State,* 1826, translated by Peter Hall. Oxford: Pergamon Press, 1966.
[97] Pages 7-11.
[98] Pages 106-156.
[99] Page 225.

100] Alfred Weber. *Theory of the Location of Industries,* translation of the 1913 edition, pages 245-252. Chicago: University of Chicago Press, 1928.

101] William Wheaton. "A Comparative Static Analysis of Urban Spatial Structure," *Journal of Economic Theory* IX: 223-237, 1974.

102] Michelle J. White. "Firm Suburbanization and Urban Subcenters," *Journal of Urban Economics* III (4): 323-343, 1976.

103] Michelle J. White. "Property Taxes and Urban Housing Abandonment." *Journal of Urban Economics* XX(3):312-330, 1986.

104] John Yinger. "Urban Models With More Than One Employment Center," pages 16-34. *Occasional Paper No. 133.* Syracuse: The Maxwell School, Syracuse University, 1989.

105] John F. Sase. *Curious Alignments: The Global Economy since 2500 BCE.* Kavish Media Books, 2009.

106] George R. Milner. *The Moundbuilders: Ancient Peoples of Eastern North America.* Thames & Hudson, 2004.

107] Henriette Mertz. *The Mystic Symbol: Mark of the Michigan Mound Builders.* Global, 1986.

108] Barry Fell. *America B.C.: Ancient Settlers in the New World.* Pocket, 1979.

109] Barry Fell. *Bronze Age America.* Little Brown & Co., 1982.

110] Wilbur B. Hinsdale. *Archeological Atlas of Michigan.* University of Michigan Press, 1932.

111] Robert J. Sharer with LOA P. TRAXLER. *The Ancient Maya* (6th (fully revised) ed.). Stanford university Press, 2006.

112] A. Vranich. "The Construction and Reconstruction of Ritual Space at Tiwanaku, Bolivia: A.D. 500-1000." *Journal of Field Archeology* 31(2): 121-136, 2006.

113] Hiram Bingham. *Machu Picchu, a Citadel of the Incas.* Hacker, 1930.

114] Robin Heath and John Michell. *The Lost Science of Measuring the Earth: Discovering the Sacred Geometry of the Ancients.* Adventures Unlimited Press, 2006.

115] Carmen M. Reinhart and Kenneth S. Rogoff. *This Time is Different: Eight Centuries of Financial Folly.* Princeton University Press, 2009.

116] Sidney Homer. *A History of Interest Rates.* Wiley, 1963.

117] Rudolf Steiner. *Knowledge of the Higher Worlds and Its Attainment.* G. P. Putnam's Sons, 1923.

118] Michael Hudson "How Interest Rates Were Set, 2500 BC to 1000 AD." *Journal of the Economics and Social History of the Orient,* Vol. 43, Spring 2000.

119] Joseph A. Schumpeter. *Business Cycles: A Theoretical, Historical and Statistical Analysis of the Capitalist Process.* McGraw-Hill, 1939.

120] Jay W. Forrester. *Urban Dynamics.* MIT Press, 1969.

121] Jay W. Forrester. *Collected Papers of Jay W. Forrester,* Productivity Press, 1975.

122] John Micklethwait and Adrian Wooldridge. *The Company: A Short History of a Revolutionary Idea,* Modern Library, 2005.

123] Adam Smith. *An Inquiry into the Nature and Causes of the Wealth of Nations.* W. Strahan and T. Cadell, 1776.

124] Robert B. Reich. *Supercapitalism: The Transformation of Business, Democracy, and Everyday Life.* Knopf, 2007.

125] Benjamin Graham. *Security Analysis*. McGraw-Hill, 1934.

126] Wilbur B. Hinsdale. *Primitive Man in Michigan*. University of Michigan Press, 1925.

127] Douglass Houghton and Bela Hubbard. *The First Geological Survey of Michigan*. 1837-1845.

128] *U.S. Geological Survey Maps of 1915*. U.S. Geological Survey. www.usgs.gov.

129] Great Lakes Global Freight Gateway (GLGFG) www.glgfg.com

130] Center for Automotive Research (C.A.R.). www.cargroup.org.

Author Index

GENERAL INDEX

absolute and relative quantities, - 88 -

administration, - 43 -

agglomeration diminish with distance, - 99 -

agglomeration economies, - 16 -, - 17 -, - 18 -, - 21 -, - 44 -, - 46 -, - 64 -, - 67 -, - 92 -, - 95 -, - 101 -, - 104 -, - 106 -, - 182 -, - 188 -

agglomeration model, - 21 -, - 67 -, - 93 -

agglomeration of unlike activities, - 92 -

agglomeration results, - 96 -

agglomerative, - 11 -, - 13 -, - 14 -, - 22 -, - 45 -, - 57 -, - 62 -, - 92 -, - 178 -, - 181 -

aggregate of firms, - 97 -

aggregation process, - 97 -

agricultural land, - 42 -

agricultural sector, - 74 -

agricultural transportation, - 53 -

agricultural workers, - 40 -

algebra, - 35 -

allegorical city, - 18 -, - 35 -, - 36 -, - 45 -, - 46 -, - 64 -

analysis of rent, - 18 -, - 64 -

ancient, - 13 -, - 14 -, - 15 -, - 16 -, - 25 -, - 27 -, - 28 -, - 29 -, - 34 -, - 35 -, - 39 -, - 44 -, - 45 -, - 46 -, - 48 -, - 58 -, - 186 -, - 187 -, - 191 -, - 193 -, - 215 -

ancient Greeks, - 29 -

ancient models, - 29 -

ancient mythology, - 29 -

ancient traditions, - 26 -

ancient variations, - 13 -, - 15 -, - 27 -

anthropology, - 14 -, - 28 -

anti-logs of densities, - 110 -, - 163 -

antiquarian sources, - 28 -

archeology, - 28 -

artificial pleasantries, - 77 -

Atlanta, - 158 -, - 161 -, - 171 -, - 174 -, - 176 -

augmentation of the business subcenter, - 107 -

average distances, - 24 -, - 168 -, - 183 -

average employment density, - 168 -, - 183 -

average estimated density, - 24 -, - 168 -, - 183 -

average sales density, - 24 -, - 168 -, - 183 -

average sales density at the CBD, - 24 -, - 168 -, - 183 -

avoidance rent phase, - 87 -

avoidance rent segment, - 70 -, - 83 -

avoidance-rent, - 20 -, - 67 -, - 85 -, - 93 -, - 106 -, - 181 -, - 246 -, - 247 -

avoidance-rent segment, - 21 -, - 67 -

Baltimore, - 158 -, - 252 -, - 255 -, - 257 -

bidding, - 18 -, - 19 -, - 20 -, - 64 -, - 65 -, - 66 -, - 68 -, - 70 -, - 83 -, - 87 -, - 89 -, - 94 -, - 105 -, - 106 -, - 181 -

Bidding, - 3 -, - 19 -, - 66 -

bid-rent, - 19 -, - 20 -, - 21 -, - 65 -, - 66 -, - 67 -, - 68 -, - 69 -, - 71 -, - 72 -, - 73 -, - 74 -, - 79 -, - 83 -, - 87 -, - 101 -, - 106 -, - 108 -, - 181 -

bid-rent functions, - 19 -

bid-rent surface, - 80 -

Made in the USA
Monee, IL
21 January 2020

20637741R00136